The Junk-Man & Other Poems by

CW01083401

Richard Thomas Gallienne was born in Liverpool on 20th Janu

After leaving school he added the 'Le' to his name. His first jo
was quickly abandoned to pursue his first love as a profession
Sonnets, was published in 1887.

In 1889 he became, for a brief time, literary secretary to Wilson Barrett the manager, actor, and
playwright. Barrett enjoyed immense success with the staging of melodramas, which would later
reach a peak with the historical tragedy The Sign of the Cross (1895).

Le Gallienne joined the staff of The Star newspaper in 1891, and also wrote for various other papers
under the pseudonym 'Logroller'. He contributed to the short-lived but influential quarterly
periodical The Yellow Book, published between 1894 and 1897.

His first wife, Mildred Lee, died in 1894 leaving their daughter, Hesper, in his care.

In 1897 he married the Danish journalist Julie Norregard. However, the marriage would not be a
success. She left him in 1903 and took their daughter Eva to live in Paris. They were eventually
divorced in June 1911.

Le Gallienne now moved to the United States and became resident there.

On 27th October 1911, he married Mrs. Irma Perry, whose marriage to her first cousin, the painter
and sculptor Roland Hinton Perry, had been dissolved in 1904. Le Gallienne and Irma had known
each other for many years and had written an article together a few years earlier in 1906.

Le Gallienne and Irma lived in Paris from the late 1920s, where Irma's daughter Gwen was by then
an established figure in the expatriate bohème. Le Gallienne also added a regular newspaper
column to the frequent publication of his poems, essays and other articles.

By 1930 Le Gallienne's book publishing career had virtually ceased. During the latter years of that
decade Le Gallienne lived in Menton on the French Riviera and, during the war years, in nearby
Monaco. His house was commandeered by German troops and his handsome library was nearly sent
back to Germany as bounty. Le Gallienne managed a successful appeal to a German officer in
Monaco which allowed him to return to Menton to collect his books.

To his credit Le Gallienne refused to write propaganda for the local German and Italian authorities,
and financially was often in dire need. On one occasion he collapsed in the street due to hunger.

Richard Thomas Gallienne died on 15th September 1947. He is buried in Menton in a grave whose
lease is, at present, due to expire in 2023.

Index of Contents

BALLADE OF THE JUNK-MAN

Upon the summer afternoon,
Wafted across the orchard trees,
There comes a ghostly travelling tune,
Blent with the sleepy drone of bees;
Elfin, aerial it is.
Like shaken bells of silver rain.
And creepy as old melodies—
The junk-man's coming down the lane.

The ancient hat, the worn-out shoon,
The broken-hearted fineries.
The yellowed news, dead as the moon.
The rust, the rubbish, and the lees.
The tarnished trophy, gallantries
Gone to the moth—this clouded cane!
This buckle brave!—for such as these
The junk-man's coming down the lane.

O thou that wooest deep in June,
Hearken! and thou so fain to seize
Joy, and to hoard it, late and soon,
Thou lord of many locks and keys,
Thick lies the dust—though no man sees—
Upon thy dream; Time sees it plain
On the bright wings, long ere it flies:
The junk-man's coming down the lane.

ENVOI

Prince, 'tis a thought our veins to freeze:
Time doth all hallowed things profane,
And toss about the centuries—
The junk-man's coming down the lane.

BALLADE OF A DEAD LADY

All old fair things are in their places,
I count them over, and miss but one;
The April flowers are running races,
The green world stretches its arms to the sun;
The nuptial dance of the days is begun—
The same young stars in the same old skies;
And all that was lost again is won—
But where have they hidden those great eyes?

All have come back—dogwood and daisies—
All things ripple and riot and run;
Swallow and swallow in aery mazes,
A fairy frolic of fire and fun;
The same old enchanted web is spun.
With diamond dews, for the same old flies;
Yet all is new, spite of Solomon—
But where have they hidden those great eyes?

Lovely as love are the new-born faces—
God knows they are fair to look upon;
And my heart goes out to the young embraces,
To the flight of the young to the young;
But, Time, what is it that thou hast done?
For my heart 'mid all the blossom cries:
"Roses are many, the Rose is gone—
Ah! where have they hidden those great eyes?"

ENVOI

Prince, I bring you my April praises.
But O on my heart a shadow lies;
For a face 1 see not all my gaze is—
Ah! where have they hidden those great eyes?

BALLADE OF THE SORROW OF YOUNG HEARTS

When I behold the sorrow of young hearts,
So innocently wild, so blindly true,
Unschooled to Life and all its weary arts,

(We that so differently wear our rue!)
These tears so fresh, these mortal wounds so new,
This loss no other heart hath ever known,
This sky so black that was so madly blue,—
In grief for this I quite forget my own.

Ah! when young lover from young lover parts,
(When I, beloved, that day did part from you!)
What balsam is there for that smart of smarts?
Alas! Time shall assuage that sorrow too;
On Young Despair there lingers still the dew,
It knows not yet the grief of grief out-grown,
That bitterest potion Time hath yet to brew—
In grief for this I quite forget my own.

Twin huntsmen Love and Death, twin poisoned darts,—
Yet Time a leech-craft to out-wit them knew;
Alas! the splendid pain too soon departs;
That fearful labyrinth without a clue
Familiar grows, and all in vain we strew
New graves for Love and Death with mimic moan,
We Life hath numbed with living through and through—
In grief for this I quite forget my own.

ENVOI

Prince, would our lovely griefs were yet to do,—
To be with our first dead again alone.
Again for love to break our hearts in two!—
In grief for this 1 quite forget my own.

BALLADE OF THE DEATHS OF KINGS

The tears of youth are even as the dew,
Up runs the laughing sun and they are dry,
Youth's broken heart breaks but a month or two,
And all the rest is a poetic sigh;
I have watched many a young perfection die,
Maids in their bloom and songsters with their strings,
But nothing half so sad beneath the sky
As the great dying of great queens and kings.

They dream on all the mighty world they knew.
Throned still and crowned, while princelings pass them by,
Strutting in brief magnificence of thew,
Scorning the wisdom of that kingly eye;
And some queen's waiting-maid, with honeyed thigh.
Titters around these poor old withered things—
I have heard nothing with so sad a cry

As the great dying of great queens and kings.

But once I caught a glance the old queen threw
To her old lord, so soft and sweet and shy,
That seemed to say, "Beloved, they dream it new
This world we have loved and fought in, you and I!"
Thereon the old king drew her to him nigh,
And—"Lovelier than April!" low he sings;
"You more a king!"—nothing can Time defy
As the great dying of great queens and kings.

ENVOI

Prince, does your wisdom know a sillier lie
Than all these shallow modern vapourings,
Or any loss to turn the world awry
As the great dying of great queens and kings?

BALLADE OF THE UNCHANGING BEAUTY

On every wind there comes the dolorous cry
Of change, and rumour vast of fair things sped.
And old perfections loudly doomed to die;
Axes agleam and running torches red.
And voices shrilling, "The old world is dead!"
Yet little heed to all this noise I pay.
But lift my eyes where, walking overhead,
The moon goes silently upon her way.

For what concern with all this change have I,
Knowing the same wild words of old were said?
For change, too, changes not; yea, this old sky
Watches mankind the same vain pathway tread.
So long ago thrones crashed, and nations bled.
Yet the old world stole back at close of day,
And on the morrow men rose up to wed—
The moon goes silently upon her way.

Abbess of all yon cloistered worlds on high,
Upon my heart your benediction shed,
Help me to put the idle turmoil by,
And on the changeless be my spirit fed;
O be my footsteps on that pathway led
Where Beauty steals among the stars to pray;
And, sorrowing earth, in this be comforted—
The moon goes silently upon her way.

ENVOI

Prince, toss not too uneasy on your bed.
Fearing your little crown be reft away;
Wear this undying wreath I weave instead—
The moon goes silently upon her way.

BALLADE OF THE BELOVED AND THE VAIN ONES THAT PERISH

When I behold the strutting pride
Of little fames that take the air,
Midget immortals, fain to stride
As those the deathless laurel wear.
Only of their poor selves aware,
And of the little things they do,
Nosing for incense everywhere,—
I smile. Beloved, and think of you.

Or when, divinely satisfied
With her brief self that seems so fair,
Turning her head from side to side,
The solemn priestess of her hair,
As she the Trojan Helen were,
Fairer than Paris ever knew,
I watch yon fleeting beauty there—
I smile. Beloved, and think of you.

Of you that laugh yourself aside.
Nor for the common plaudits care,
And neither advertise nor hide
All that is you, with more to spare,
So nonchalantly past compare,—
You hear the vocal vain ones through,
Nor ever dream to claim your share—
I smile, Beloved, and think of you.

ENVOI

Princess, not this nor yet next year
Shall genius, mirth, and beauty too
Be found in such conjunction rare—
I smile, Beloved, and think of you.

BALLADE OF ANNETTE

'Tis not for me to doubt her wonder,
I quite believe each word you say;
In fact, I think you rather under—
Than over-praise your "fiancee";

'Tis no mere compliment I pay.
In her, I see, all charms are met,
As lovely as the month of May:
But tell me—have you seen Annette?

A beauty without blot or blunder,
A thing of dew and dawn and spray;
A dove high up against the thunder
Were not so white and far away;
Her face—well, you just want to pray!
Too lovely to believe, and yet
A woman—woman all the way:
Ah! tell me—have you seen Annette?

The wild bees, weighted down with plunder,
Wise in all blossom, even they
Find no flower like her lips asunder;
And who should in her bosom stray,
And taste that honey, falleth fey
Forever—ne'er shall he forget
The sweetness till his dying day:
Ah! tell me—have you seen Annette?

ENVOI

Prince, should you see her—lack-a-day!
Deep in your castle's oubliette
Were I—she is so fair a prey:
Ah! tell me—have you seen Annette?

BALLADE OF THE BREAKING OF HEARTS

Singers and brothers learned in the lore
Of loving of fair faces, and all ye
That love one lady, and one lady more;
Yea! count not on two hands your gallantry,
So moved to all of lovesome shape are ye.
Ever with longing fain that finds no rest,

I pray you answer this sad word for me:
Why do we break the heart we love the best?

Dead men had knowledge of this heretofore,
Even the lords of Love's high chivalry
Whose names still, darkened not, in heaven soar;
Lancelot and Tristan knew this perfidy,
Though never man had such immortal She;
'Twas not enough God gave His loveliest.

To save their mortal eyes from glamory—
Why do we break the heart we love the best?

Yet true—one hallowed face we but adore,
Of our heart's treasure hers alone the key,
And, should God take her, ever at His door
We knock with anguish through Eternity,
In hell forever once her face to see,
Seeking it ever in a fearful quest,
'Tis a strange riddle I propose, perdie,—
Why do we break the heart we love the best?

ENVOI

God, that hath all sad mortal men in fee,
O why, with witchcraft hair and lunar breast,
Hast Thou encompassed us with sorcery?
Why do we break the heart we love the best?

BALLADE OF QUEEN'S LACE

Go not to marts of costly show
To clothe those limbs so round and fair,
But let us to the woodlands go—
I'll find you prettier things to wear.
Hung in a magic wardrobe there;
Garlands to frame your fairy face.
And misty lawns as fine as air,
And for your petticoat Queen's Lace.

Soft draperies of virgin snow,
If you must hide that bosom rare,
Whiter than Helen's long ago—
'Twere kinder, love, to leave it bare.
Dimmed only by your falling hair,—
Yet, if you must deny that grace,
Lo! veils of filmiest gossamer—

And for your petticoat Queen's Lace.
And flounce and frill and furbelow,
Quaint dimity and diaper,
The fairy artists shape and sew;
Here's silk-weed for your stomacher.
And round that sweet diameter
Yclept your waist this girdle place—
Diana wore the same I swear!
And for your petticoat Queen's Lace.

ENVOI

Princess, and ladies everywhere.
Fashion but ill your form displays;
Nature's your best costumier—
And for your petticoat Queen's Lace.

BALLADE OF HIS LADY'S IMMORTALITY

O summer day, all hot with bee and rose,
Heavy with honey, like a cup of gold
A-brim with the wild wine that overflows
The limits of the world—ah! love, we hold
The cup awhile and drink, as they of old
Before us, drinking thus, 'neath the same sky;
As we they laughed, then fell a-sudden cold—
But you are far too beautiful to die.

Fair face, wherein Life's colour softly glows,
Flower that within your petals, fold on fold,
Hoards from the sun your sanctuary snows,
Dazzlingly hid from lovers over-bold;
As the young moon, high up above the wold,
Grants but a gleam of whiteness to the eye
That fain would have her silver all unfold—
But you are far too beautiful to die.

The moon will set, the fairest flower dose,
This summer day be like a screed up-rolled,
Or soon or late the lingering glory goes,
Or soon or late the noblest tale is told;
Yours is a loveliness too manifold
For sacrilegious death even to deny;
All other fairness turns to fragrant mould—
But you are far too beautiful to die.

ENVOI

Princess, fear not the passage to behold
Of Beauty, living but in song or sigh,
For others must the passing-bell be tolled—
But you are far too beautiful to die.

BALLADE OF THE SINGING STREAM

When June is back, and earth is kind,—
'Tis long, this winter day, perdie!—
And frost and snow are left behind,

And leaves are green upon the tree,
And happy lives of bird and bee
Sport in the re-awakened beam.
Love, I appoint a tryst with thee—
At the Sign of the Singing Stream.

O come upon the summer wind.
And bring thy blue eyes like the sea,
And all thy long bright hair unbind,
Wafting its fragrance out to me,
Leave all thy whiteness wild and free,
And like a woodland dryad gleam—
Love only shall be there to see,
At the Sign of the Singing Stream.

Then we the leafy grot shall find,
The rose-embowered sanctuary,
Where hangs the fruit with golden rind,
And we shall eat right merrily,
And as the immortal gods shall be,
Glad children of the cosmic dream.
Transfigured with felicity—
At the Sign of the Singing Stream.

ENVOI

Princess, the solemn stars decree,
As part of the celestial scheme,
This tryst, whereof we keep the key
At the Sign of the Singing Stream.

BALLADE OF THE NOISINESS OF THE TIMES

O what a noisy world it is!
Such shriek of news—yet nothing new;
Or is it I that am amiss,
Or does it seem the same to you?
"If peace" meant only "quiet" too!
Behind the times I know I am,
But what is a tired man to do?
I light my pipe, and read Charles Lamb.

So small our gain, so much we miss,
For still the old remains the true,
And Solomon on novelties
Spake even wiser than he knew;
With all our feverish to-do,
Air-ship and wireless telegram,
Life's much the same,—and, entre nous,

I light my pipe, and read Charles Lamb.

Though names may change from That to This,
The "historic times we're living through"
Were writ in ancient histories;
It is the same old human brew,
With just a little change or two;
Our progress is the same old sham—
The same old ship, the same old crew—
I light my pipe, and read Charles Lamb.

ENVOI

Prince, bide your time, be not too blue,
Though you the "Soviets" bedamn,—
The world is not quite all yahoo;
Just light your pipe, and read Charles Lamb.

BALLADE OF THE POET AND THE MOON

The day has gone of lovely things,
According to the modern bard;
Of dreariness and dross he sings,
And hymns the homely and the hard,
The sweat-shop and the engine yard;
Of these he makes his doleful tune.
And plenteous slang doth interlard—
I still prefer to sing the moon.

Dry are the Heliconian springs.
And sere is Enna flower-bestarred;
Speak not of Pegasus his wings,
For all such ancientry is barred,—
Yea! feathered shalt thou be and tarred
For such old nonsense in thy rune,—
By Heloise and Abelard,
I still prefer to sing the moon.

Nor dare to speak of queens and kings,
Democracy is now the card;
On the fair Past the poet flings
The flint, the pebble and the shard;
The gospels of the Savoyard
Have wrought this sans-culottish boon,—
O for some frankincense and nard!
I still prefer to sing the moon.

ENVOI

Ah! Prince—or rather I mean "pard"—
Let's to our lotus and lagoon,
And call for our Pretorian guard:
I still prefer to sing the moon.

BALLADE OF APOLLO'S GARDEN

Friend, in the storm and stress of things,
Art thou aweary, even as I?
Wouldst flee the noisy fall of kings?
From all the wrath and rabble fly?
A shelter is forever nigh,
Tranquil with dews and green to see,
A place of songs that cannot die—
The garden with the golden key.

Here leap the Heliconian springs.
The sacred fountains never dry;
Apollo, with his golden strings,
Over the grass goes wandering by;
And wild-rose breast and marble thigh—
Goddess, or nymph immortal, she—
Haunt, fleeing the ensorcelled eye,
The garden with the golden key.

Needs but one charmed line that sings.
Thou canst the roaring loom defy;
For wide the magic portal swings,
And Homer takes thee to his sky,
And laughing Shakespeare bids thee lie
A dream beneath his greenwood tree,
Far from the hurrying hue and cry—
The garden with the golden key.

ENVOI

Prince, dost thou seek to dulcify
Thy bitter lot? Wouldst sanctuary
And surcease find? I make reply,
"The garden with the golden key."

A BALLADE-CATALOGUE OF LOVELY THINGS

I would make a list against the evil days
Of lovely things to hold in memory:
First, I set down my lady's lovely face,
For earth has no such lovely thing as she;

And next I add, to bear her company,
The great-eyed virgin star that morning brings;
Then the wild-rose upon its little tree—
So runs my catalogue of lovely things.

The enchanted dog-wood, with its ivory trays,
The water-lily in its sanctuary
Of reeded pools, and dew-drenched lilac sprays,
For these, of all fair flowers, the fairest be;
Next write I down the great name of the sea.
Lonely in greatness as the names of kings;
Then the young moon that hath us all in fee—
So runs my catalogue of lovely things.

Imperial sunsets that in crimson blaze
Along the hills, and, fairer still to me,
The fireflies dancing in a netted maze
Woven of twilight and tranquillity;
Shakespeare and Virgil, their high poesy;
Then a great ship, splendid with snowy wings,
Voyaging on into eternity—
So runs my catalogue of lovely things.

ENVOI

Prince, not the gold bars of thy treasury,
Not all thy jewelled sceptres, crowns and rings,
Are worth the honeycomb of the wild bee—
So runs my catalogue of lovely things.

BALLADE OF THE HANGING GARDENS OF BABYLON

The fierce queen wearied, and she smote her hands:
"Summon my lord, the King," she spake and sighed,
"I sicken of these steaming shallow lands!"
Nebuchadnezzar stood there by her side,
Suppliant. She turned upon him, eagle-eyed;
"O King, would thou and Babylon ne'er had been!

I die for pines and storms." "Amytis, bride,
There shall be hanging gardens for my queen."

"O for Assyria, where each mountain stands,
With pine-trees to the peak, and the great stride
Of the north wind, voiced as a god's commands.
Shakes forests into music far and wide,
Iron and granite song; and horsemen ride
By foam of torrents, laughing, lances keen—
But I mid ooze and baking bricks must bide. . . ."

"There shall be hanging gardens for my queen."

Night fell, and morning rose with crimson bands,
About her couch the tiring maidens glide.
And one that wove her hair in shining strands
Spake softly: "Vouch, great queen, to gaze outside,
Beyond the curtains"—and Amytis cried,
And laughed and wept for what her eyes had seen—
Assyria at her window magnified!—
"There shall be hanging gardens for my queen."

ENVOI

"Queen," spake the King, "is thy heart satisfied?
Unnumbered slaves and Night have wrought this scene—
The rocks and pines of thy Assyrian pride:
There shall be hanging gardens for my queen."

A BOOKMAN'S BALLADE OF "THE BIG THREE"

Have you, as I, O Reader kind,
Sometimes before your bookshelves stood,
Seeking in vain some book to find,
The proper and peculiar food
For some un je-ne-sais-quot mood?—
In other words, you know not what—
May I advise, yet not intrude,
Dickens, Dumas, or Walter Scott?

With all fair fruitage of the mind.
The beautiful, the wise, the good,
Your shelves luxuriously are lined;
And yet, O strange ingratitude!
They bring you no beatitude,
The charm they had this day is not:
Try, then—if I were you, I should
Dickens, Dumas, or Walter Scott.

For idle "vapours" undefined,
For sickly Thought's distempered brood,
Throw "psycho-analysts" behind
The fire, and be all such eschewed:
Let simple laughter stir your blood,
And plot, and breathless counter-plot,
And all Life's moving multitude—
Dickens, Dumas, or Walter Scott.

ENVOI

Yea, gentle Reader, if we would
Forget ourselves, our cares forgot,
None else can equal, by the Rood,
Dickens, Dumas, or Walter Scott.

BALLADE OF PESSIMISTS

(Dedicated to the Little Masters of Decay)

Pessimists all, all ye that swear
By Nietzsche, Freud, and Edgar Poe,
Remy de Gourmont, Baudelaire,
And Gabriele D'Annunzio,
And other gentlemen of woe,—
All that is nasty, "strange" and "new"—
I'd like—and yet not like!—to know.
If Life's all wrong,—what's wrong with you?

You that pollute the wholesome air
With nauseous pullulating flow
From brains unclean and sick despair,
Doting on dirt, and footing slow
Where leprous-spotted fungi grow,
Abhorring all the gold and blue
Where morning sings and brave winds blow;
If Life's all wrong—what's wrong with you?

O world that Shakespeare found so fair,
This goodly and most gallant show,
This bannered, flower-strewn thoroughfare
Where Life and Love in glory go,
And Courage Sorrow doth o'er-crow,
And Wonder, with perpetual dew;
For me the world is well enow:
If Life's all wrong—what's wrong with you?

ENVOI

To Hades, Prince, these caitiffs throw,
Rat-poison for the sickly crew
That reap not, neither do they sow!
If Life's all wrong—what's wrong with you?

BALLADE OF LIFE'S DREAM

The cry is that the world grows old,—
Though I, for one, the charge gainsay,—

That every fairy-tale is told,
And all Romance is passed away:
Believe it not, this summer day,
Better believe yon running stream
That hath this wiser thing to say—
Life's still the same old foolish dream.

Yea! let the shrill reformers scold,
And all our fond illusions flay,
Our blood refuses to run cold.
Our happy hearts know more than they,
The splendid something in our clay
Shrivels with fire their dusty theme;
Come, sweetheart, kiss we while we may—
Life's still the same old foolish dream.

Still the old earth, with blue and gold,
Laughs at the gospels of decay,
Rings to the stars its challenge bold,
And works its work, and plays its play,
What though the devil be to pay;
Living's a gay and gallant scheme,
Tis only fools that say it nay—
Life's still the same old foolish dream.

ENVOI

Lord of my Being, I humbly lay
Thanks at Thy throne, how strange it seem,
For life, that too brief holiday,
Life—still the same old foolish dream.

BALLADE OF POT-POURRI

Once more the garden leaps in fire,
The lips of June how red, how red!
But the young rose of my desire
Blooms in the garden of the dead;
Nor will she raise her dreaming head
For any song, how sweet it be—
Flame on, ye flowers in glory spread!
Bring me my jar of pot-pourri.

With brimming cup and soaring spire.
Glows and smells sweet each garden bed;
The haughty tapestries of Tyre
Never so many glories wed
Into their pomp of royal thread;
Nor ever yet hath honey-bee

On such delirious nectar fed—
Bring me my jar of pot-pourri.

Lover, that, with enamoured lyre.
Love at thy side with aery tread,
Singest in this garden, to a quire
Of answering angels overhead,
Long be it ere thy joy be sped!
Here is no fairer flower than she;
Yet mine a lovelier thing instead—
Bring me my jar of pot-pourri.

ENVOI

Prince of Life's Garden, hear it said:
However rare thy rose—shall be
More rare her hoarded petals shed:
Bring me my jar of pot-pourri.

BALLADE OF AMARYLLIS IN THE SHADE

Were it not better done—the time being Spring—
Grim poet, the iron of whose Cromwellian lyre
Is sistered with so soft a lyric string,
To cast dry wisdom crackling on the fire,
And follow the green pathways of desire,
Where April flutters like a flying maid;
Though others to the topmost stars aspire—
To sport with Amaryllis in the shade?

To rule wouldst thou?—to be the sorry king
Of this poor kingdom of the fool and liar
We call the world; or, a still stranger thing,
Wouldst swink and sweat, and house thee in the mire,
And sell thy strong soul for a captive's hire,
While tyrants eat, and hear sweet music played?
Were it not better done—who need inquire?—
To sport with Amaryllis in the shade?

While all is still new blossom and young wing,
And life's a flame still mounting higher and higher,
While still Youth's gold is thine to flaunt and fling,
Heed not dim counsels of some shrivelled sire;
Spake he but sooth, upon the funeral pyre
One dream shall linger as his ashes fade—
Of Love's plumed feet aflame through brake and brier,
To sport with Amaryllis in the shade.

ENVOI

My Prince, what better dream should man require
To close his eyes? And 1 have heard it said
That Death's a garden where we but retire—
To sport with Amaryllis in the shade.

A NEW BALLADE OF LAST YEAR'S SNOW

Villon, in French none may forget,
"What has become of last year's snow?"
You asked—nor is there answer yet;
And where did those dead ladies go
With bosoms worn exceeding low,
With hair of gold, and lips of red?
It drifted—would you really know—
Flake after flake upon my head.

Ah! suns may rise and suns may set,
Catullus told us long ago,
But, howsoe'er we fume and fret,
The wind takes all our mortal show,
And youth hath scarcely time to blow
In Life's brief garden, ere 'tis fled—
Yet why so early settle so
Flake after flake upon my head?

But yesterday my locks were jet,
Rival of raven and of crow,
Yet, while I dined with Juliet,
And passed the wine-cup to and fro,
For all the glory and the glow,
The gray was creeping thread by thread,
Falling, a soft insidious foe,
Flake after flake upon my head.

ENVOI

Ah! Prince, the sorry overthrow!
A man might just as well be dead,
When once the years begin to sow
Flake after flake upon his head.

BALLADE OF THE ROAD UNKNOWN

Let others keep the beaten track,
The straight and narrow path of fears,
Like timid travellers looking back

At any sound that meets their ears;
Shall I, because some neighbour jeers,
Follow the same dull road as he;
Or steer the coward course he steers?—
The lure of the road unknown for me.

A hickory stick, a shouldered pack,
Bread and a book, the wine that cheers,
The sun and moon for almanack,
The planets leaning on their spears,
A bush for inn as twilight nears,
And somewhere through it all the sea;
Afoot again as morning peers—
The lure of the road unknown for me.

When comes the fatal click and clack
Of Time's relentless iron shears,
When the thin ice of life goes crack,
And the black gulf beneath uprears,
And all the kind world disappears;
Still, as of old, my cry shall be,
Somewhere high up amid the spheres—'
The lure of the road unknown for me.

ENVOI

Dear Prince, the old romantic years
Were filled with glory, girls and glee;
But, though 1 love them through my tears—
The lure of the road unknown for me.

BALLADE OF OLD LAUGHTER

When I look back, as daylight closes,
And count my gains and losses o'er,
Rough with the smooth; the rue, the roses;
The lost and lovely that no more
Come when I knock upon the door,
Or even answer when I call,
I see, of all that went before.
The laughter was the best of all.

Man's life, some say, a thing of prose is;
Not so his life—as mine of yore—
Who on Miranda's breast reposes—
Ah! God, that fragrant frock she wore!
Hid honey still at the heart's core
Her bosom like a hushed snow-fall—
And yet, for all we kissed and swore,

The laughter was the best of all.

Truth after truth old Time discloses.
But, as we hobble to fourscore,
Each finds that not as he supposes
The gains for which he travailed sore:
Glory or gold, the wine we pour.
The face that held our lives in thrall—
Somehow the bravest grows a bore.
The laughter was the best of all.

ENVOI

Prince, much of wisdom heretofore
Time's patient pages doth bescrawl;
This is the sum of all our lore—
The laughter was the best of all.

BALLADE TO HIS DEAD LADY, BIDDING HER SLEEP ON

There was a time, O fairest head
That all too early sought repose,
That I could not be comforted
Until your face again arose,
And the Lord Jesu well He knows
If I have failed my troth to keep;
But now, where the tall poppy grows,
I only come to whisper "Sleep!"

So few the years since you are sped
Along the pathway of the snows,
Still are you young amid the dead;
But, since your going, the world goes
A wild way, every wind that blows
Whirls some old fairness to the deep.
And Beauty flies before her foes—
I only come to whisper "Sleep!"

Glad am I of your quiet bed,
Glad am I of the stream that flows,
Murmuring to you its drowsihead,
Glad am I of the punctual rose
That over you its petals throws,
Glad of the willow-leaves that weep
Above us both, as, leaning close,
I only come to whisper "Sleep!"

ENVOI

Princess, my heart its hope foregoes,
All that we loved away they sweep,
A world of carrion kites and crows—
I only come to whisper "Sleep!"

BALLADE OF THE THINGS THAT REMAIN

The loveliness of water, its faery ways
With cloud and wind, its myriad sorceries
With morning and the moon, and stars agaze
In its still glass, and the tranced summer trees;
The vowelled rivers, the rough-throated seas,
The tides that brim with silver the grassy plain,
Or strew lone islands with lost argosies:
We come and go—these things remain.

Fire and its gnomes, soft-talking as it plays,
Dream-like, amid its fretted imageries,
Or melting the wild hills, and with its blaze
Licking the very stars; and, even as these.
The winds that blow through all the centuries,
The falling snow, the shining April rain,
Birds singing, and the far-off Pleiades:
We come and go—these things remain.

God's glory, and the march of nights and days,
The seals upon the ancient mysteries
Of rose and star and woman's magic face,
That, seeing, man loves, yet knows not what he sees;
The old sweet sins, the old sweet sanctuaries;
War and long peace, then war and peace again;
The Dark and in Death's hands the dreadful keys:
We come and go—these things remain.

ENVOI

Prince, save ourselves, there is but little flees
That comes not back, even as this refrain;
'Faith, 'tis a thought that doth me greatly please:
We come and go—these things remain.

II

ON RE-READING LE MORTE D' ARTHUR

Here learn who will the art of noble words,
If he may snatch the secret the words keep

Of speech like new-sprung grass to nibbling herds.
Yet old as graves of long-forgotten sleep;
Bright as young joy, yet with a heart as deep
As those old wells of tears that never dry;
Alike for those who laugh or those who weep
Friendly of face as is the morning sky,
Bannered with bloom-tipt clouds lullingly moving by.

Like some green glade in middle of the wood,
Buttressed with beech and oak and arched with bowers,
Spreads the old tale in nature's amplitude,
And many a grassy corner blue with flowers;
Anon uprears a castle grim with towers,
Anon a horn is blown, in silken weeds
A lovely lady, fairer far than ours,
On a white palfrey rides, anon there speeds
A knight with vizor down, intent on flaming deeds.

Here, by a well—beware her woven charms—
A faery woman sits and softly sings,
White as shed blossom are her beckoning arms.
And in her eyes a thousand vanished springs;
She lies in wait to snare the youth of kings,
On their fair strength is all her whiteness fed,
A joy like honey in the mouth she brings,
Yet whoso tasteth it is surely sped
Down to the hollow halls of the dishonoured dead.

Of all within this Forest Perilous
Hight is the world, there is no thing to fear
Deadly as she, no giant Orgulous,
No Questing Beast, or no illustrious spear;
Yea! though the Hundred Knights should draw anear,
Better, with lance in rest, it were to fall
Than to her lonely singing to give ear;
Fame hath a voice more nobly musical,
And thus to dare to die is scarce to die at all.

Old book that still hath such a morning face,
Dust are old eyes that read thee, yet no dust
Is on the page they read; for thee no place
Where dim Oblivion turneth all to rust,
And later scrolls diurnally are thrust;
But thou of Youth art still the very friend,
And Age grows Youth to read thee—such a gust
Dwells in the glamoured page o'er which we bend,
And still we sigh that the old tale, like life, must end,

I read thee, like my fellows, in the morn,
And now the westering sun begins to throw
A pathos o'er the realm where I was born,

Touching with fire old fanes of long ago,
Re-animating with a charmed glow
Memories dim and faces fled away—
I hear again thy bannered trumpets blow,
And fall a-dream on that heraldic day
When I was a young knight and she a little may.

Gone! and yet here forever still abide,
Stored as in music, all the aching joy
And glory of young hearts that, side by side,
Beat on when she was girl and I was boy,
And the Round Table, and the Siege of Troy,
And Roland's Song, and the far wandering seas
Round Jason's keel, and all the long employ
Of Hercules, were our realities,—
Nor had we doubt to find, we two, the Hesperides.

Yea! this old book, as others writ of old,
And writ for ever, like a palimpsest,
Is over-writ with other words of gold,
Though marring not the meaning of the rest:
The words low uttered when two lovers pressed
Hot cheeks together o'er the tear-stained tale,
And the long secret was at last confessed—
And twilight wove for love a starry veil.
And silence was all speech—save for the nightingale.

Would we who write in this thought-burdened day
Seek for our words endurance such as this,
Have unborn lovers read us even as they
That read of Launcelot—then dared to kiss,
And blessed the magic book that wrought their bliss,
Forgot a moment, but remembered ever—
Somewhere in this old book the secret is:
No more, perchance, though some shall find it never,
Than—wouldst thou be immortal, be thou not too clever.

This too—the golden increment of Time—
Mark in these noble books that never die:
A mystic ripening, be it prose or rhyme,
With deeper meanings, as the years go by,
Something not there for the first reader's eye;
As though even books were part of Nature's scheme,
And, with the suns, drew something from the sky,
Thrilling with subtler sense the simple theme,
Broadening to vaster scope the artless early dream.

So, he of Mancha on his sorry steed.
Tilting at windmills, and his fellow fool,
Seemed not at first as now for us who read,—
For Man hath since so often gone to school—

And, as the weathering years make beautiful
Old stone beyond the builder's first intent,
An art of Time, past reach of skill or tool.
Makes of his book more than its author meant,
And a quaint tale becomes a people's monument.

Yet, 'tis enough—the tale as first was told,
Read with a boy's hot heart, or with a mind
To watch the blazoned narrative unfold,
And of the simple words the magic find,
Watching the art that leaves no clue behind:
Sudden as sunshine on a grassy place,
Mark how this pen, with art as undesigned.
Writes but a name, and lo! the lovely face
Of La Belle Isoud blooms with death-defying grace.

Though Gawaine's skull, and the old Table Round,
And Cradok's mantle, and Sir Launcelot
His sword—beheld of Caxton—now be found
No more at Winchester or Camelot;
And Arthur's seal, as Arthur's self, is not,
And all the lovely queens are even as they,
And Orkney hath no memory of King Lot;
And all the magic art of Nimud
Be spent, and even Merlin's dust be blown away;

Here live they still, as in that mirrored spring—
With life's own colours on them, clear to see—
Where Palamides, gazing, gan to sing
Of Isoud, for whose sake all gaunt was he,
And dared to tell Sir Tristram love was free,
And Isoud his to love, though ne'er to win,
As any man's—though he Sir Tristram be. . .
Ah! noble paynim, long since chrismed of sin,
When Tristram to Christ's font brother-like, led thee in!

"Go," said Isoud, "and tell Queen Guenevere,
That in the world there be true lovers four:
She and Sir Launcelot, and Sir Tristram here,
And I, Isoud, and on the earth no more"—
Proud boast ensuing Time hath not out-wore,
Still, like a rose upon her lips, you brave
A world un-friend to lovers as of yore,—
Writ was the whole of love the hour you gave
The golden cup to Tristram, golden to the grave.

And, in the shock of times that shake the world,
I hear no thunder in the wars men wage
As when Sir Tristram on Sir Marhaus hurled—
Writ is the whole of battle in that page;
Yet, whatsoe'er of glory gilds the rage

Of metal, soul-less, upon metal flung,
Springs from this noble England's heritage,
This book of England's knights in England's tongue,
When her great speech and her great heart alike were young.

Nor, when man's heart beneath the Unseen bows,
And the dread holiness that hidden dwells
In being bends the knee, and in God's house
A light passes, and the sound of mystic bells,
And man is ware of opening heavens and hells,
Shall he such vision have as the pure lad
Of whose hushed quest the old romancer tells,—
All, all is here, all lovely good and bad;
God too is in the book—with young Sir Galahad.

III

A BAHAMAN LOVE-SONG

The morning like a river runs
With feet of music through the palms,
Come match your glory with the sun's,
And breathe with me a thousand balms;
The dawn is like an azure door
Flung open wide for us to flee,
And watch along the surf-ringed shore
The heaving jewel of the sea.

And we will find some coral cave,
Where you shall doff your linen fair.
By the foam-lipped up-running wave,
And free the marvel of your hair,
And match your whiteness with the spray,
And match your strange eyes with the sea,
And, like a nereid, you shall sway
Cradled in lapis-lazuli;

Then turn and, like a dolphin, glide
Through hollow halls of glimmering jade.
Where solemn gleaming fish abide
For ever in a twilight glade;
And I shall watch you sink and pass,
Then dive, and mid-way we shall meet,
Two dreams within a magic glass
That join dim lips with sea-salt sweet.

Then shall we hoist a snowy sail,
And, in a boat with crystal floor,
Gaze down on shapes in rainbow mail,

Star-fish and branching madrepore.
And peacock fans and faery flowers
That in a mystic garden dream,
Of moon-white sands and coral bowers,
Tranced deep in the pellucid stream.

There might I dwell as in your eyes,
And never to the world return—
But lo! another Paradise
Of beckoning palms and tropic fern—
Yon island ringed with sun-kissed foam:
O let us there our boat careen,
And I will build our hidden home,
And you shall be the island queen.

And I will serve you, morn and eve,
Of golden fruits shall be our fare,
And garlands for your body weave,
And dive for pearls, to deck your hair;
And Love shall be the island laws,
Love all its business, all its play,
The world and all its silly saws
A foolish legend far away.

THE ETERNAL FRIENDS

Is it not very strange that you and I,
That once had never heard the other's name,
Knowing not either lived beneath the sky,
At last mysteriously to each other came.
Suddenly close and near that were so far,
Two grown to one as stalk and flower are?

I was on earth before you, knew the spring
While you still slept in heaven, the white bloom
Of April, and all things that bud and sing—
As though the world were making fair a room
For you to step in from your cradling sphere,
Nor find it too unlovely to be here.

When your white feet first touched our earthly shore,
Surely some shock of sweetness trembled through
The leafy world, as morn the message bore
Over the glittering gardens, singing—You;
Yet heard I not—and the long years sped by,
But of your lovely face no news had I.

O idle years that kept us thus apart,
Walking, as in a maze, so late to find,

That else had been one history, heart to heart;
Yet not in vain perchance those years behind—
For thus slow Time, 'gainst Love's impatience wise.
Prepared our souls to meet each other's eyes.

Beloved apparition, ghostly fair,
Divinely new, and yet for ever known,
So strangely come to me out of the air—
How wondrously familiar hath Love grown
Since that far day; yet ever stranger too
The marvel of this magic life with you.

Strange to know such a flower for very friend,
With the young moon, day in, day out, to dwell,
A shining comrade to the journey's end:
End where it will, with her it must be well;
And, as she touches each small common thing
Of life—Ah! how it learns to bloom and sing.

Whether the road we tread be dust or dew,
Menaced with storm, or lit with pearl and rose,
'Tis a good road together, and we two
Follow it, singing—^whither the road goes
Content to know not, so, where'er it wends,
We fare it always thus—immortal friends.

LOVE'S MIRROR

Be thou my mirror, love, that I may see
Myself transfigured in the light of thee,—
Ah! I have need to see my face as thou
Deemest it is—or feignest it to be.
And I! what can I bring? yet this will I:
Out of my reverence I will build a dome,
Where the wide sorrow of the world shall bow
In prayer, and in the thought of thee find rest.
And in thy smile the homeless find a home;
The incense of the lilies of thy breast
Shall be a balm upon them, and each caress
Thou givest me shall all the nations bless.

Out of our joy—lo! I will build a dream
Of lovely words, where all may enter in.
And bathe their weariness as in a stream.
And put away all sorrow and all sin.
Ah! but the heart of it shall all be ours,
Shut in amid a holiness of flowers,
My heart to yours for ever, and my lips
On yours for ever, as the base world slips

Away from us—and nought but thou and I
Alone, we two, with God, until we die.

ANNIVERSARY

This day of ours
Is still our day;
Immortal flowers,
And fadeless bay,
Crown it; though tears
Be on them now.
The faithful years.
The heart's own vow,
Stand firm behind
Us as of old—
Still are you, love,
My girl of gold!
Still shall the sun,
Upon his way,
Bring us his blessing
On this day;
And still the moon,
With faery beams,
Hallow the house
We built of dreams.

AUBADE

Under the roof in the valley yonder
Lies the head all made of wonder,
Sleeping yet,
Dreaming yet:
For why should she wake, when the dawn scarce stirs,
With her star-crowned head still asleep as hers;
And only the birds and I are awake,
To sing for her sake.

O teach me a song, you morning bird,
For me to take back to her, word for word,
To sing as she lifts each mighty lid,
Heavy with sleep as a pyramid:
Put into the song all the love of my heart—
A man's love, with a wild bird's art.

TO A CELESTIAL HOUSE-WIFE

O hills, I would that you might bathe her brows
In your high balm;
Too many little matters of the house
Destroy her calm.

She must be gay while others fume and fret,
And, all day long.
The business of her own deep soul forget,
With merry tongue.

Would that on her this brook, with morning spell,
Might lay its hand,
Talking with liquid lulling syllable
Through the green land.

She has sore need of these immortal things,
So blue and still;
To sit her down by the eternal springs,
And drink her fill.

SONG FOR A GOWN

I went into the woods to make a song,
Wherewith to buy with words my love a gown;
And, scarce had I but entered, the wild rose
Threw all her blossoms down.

Yea! April stripped her virgin body bare,
Standing all naked in the morning shine,
Robbed her sweet self of all her raiment fair,
To clothe that love of mine.

Then, lost in looking, almost I forgot
My purpose coming to that woody place;
Yea! almost I forgot to make my song,
Gazing on April's face.

WHEN ALL THE DREAMS ARE OVER

When all the dreams are over,
And all the long day done,
And we no longer heed the stern
Reveille of the sun;

I wonder, love, if you will be
A bird that skims and skims

The grasses, or a little fish
That swims and swims and swims.

Or will you be a blue-eyed flower,
And grow just over me,
And we will talk together
Of all that used to be.

IV

THE PALACES OF THE ROSE

A Valentine

Which of my palaces? Gold one by one,
Of all the splendid houses of my throne,
This day in grave thought have I over-gone:
Those roofs of stars where I have lived alone
Gladly with God; those blue-encompassed bowers
Hushed round with lakes, and guarded with still flowers,
Where I have watched a face from eve till morn,
Wondering at being born—
Then on from morn again till the next eve,
Still with strange eyes, unable to believe;
And yet, though week and month and year went by,
Incredulous of my ensorcelled eye.
O had I thus in trance for ever stayed.
Still were she there in the reed-girdled isle.
And I there still—I who go treading now
Eternity, a-hungered mile by mile:
Because I pressed one kiss upon her brow,—
After a thousand years that seemed an hour
Of looking on my flower,
After that patient planetary fast,
One kiss at last;
One kiss—and then strange dust that once was she.

Sayest thou, Rose, "What is all this to me?"
This would I answer, if it pleaseth thee.
Thou Rose and Nightingale so strangely one:
That of my palaces, gold one by one,
I fell a-thinking, pondering which to-day,
The day of the Blessed saint Saint Valentine,
Which of those many palaces of mine,
I, with bowed head and lowly bended knee.
Might bring to thee.
O which of all my lordly roofs that rise.
To kiss the starry skies,
May with great beams make safe that golden head,

With all that treasure of hair showered and spread,
Careless as though it were not gold at all—
Yet in the midnight lighting the black hall;
And all that whiteness lying there, as though
It were but driven snow.

Pondering on all these pinnacles and towers,
That, as I come with trumpets, call me lord,
And crown their battlements with girlhood flowers,
I can but think of one. 'Twas not my sword
That won it, nor was it aught I did or dreamed,
But O it is a palace worthy thee!
For all about it flows the eternal sea,
A blue moat guarding an immortal queen;
And over it an everlasting crown
That, as the moon comes and the sun goes down,
Adds jewel after jewel, gem on gem,
To the august appropriate diadem
Of her, in whom all potencies that are
Wield sceptres and with quiet hands control;
Kind as that fairy wand the evening star,
Or the strong angel that we call the soul.

Thou splendid girl that seemest the mother of all,
Dear Ceres-Aphrodite, with every lure
That draws the bee to honey, with the call
Of moth-winged night to sinners, yet as pure
As the white nun that counts the stars for beads;
Thou blest Madonna of all broken needs,
Thou Melusine, thou sister of sorrowing men,
Thou wave-like laughter, thou dear sob in the throat,
Thou all-enfolding mercy, and thou song
That gathers up each wild and wandering note.
And takes and breaks and heals and breaks the heart
With the omnipotent tenderness of art;
And thou Intelligence of rose-leaves made
That makes that little thing the brain afraid.

For thee my Castle of the Spring prepares:
On the four winds are sped my couriers,
For thee the towered trees are hung with green;
Once more for thee, O queen,
The banquet hall with ancient tapestry
Of woven vines grows fair and still more fair.
And ah! how in the minstrel gallery
Again there is the sudden string and stir
Of music touching the old instruments.
While on the ancient floor
The rushes as of yore
Nymphs of the house of spring plait for your feet—
Ancestral ornaments.

And everywhere a hurrying to and fro,
And whispers saying, "She is so sweet—so sweet";
O violets, be ye not too late to blow,
O daffodils be fleet:
For, when she comes, all must be in its place,
All ready for her entrance at the door,
All gladness and all glory for her face,
All flowers for her flower-feet a floor;
And, for her sleep at night in that great bed
Where her great locks are spread,
O be ye ready, ye young woodland streams,
To sing her back her dreams.

SWEET LOVERS

(For Gwen and André)

Sweet lovers!
Don't you think I know
This is the hour—
The dawn's aglow,
The world's aflower,
Sweet lovers!

Sweet lovers!
Listen, were I you,
I'd be away
Across the dew,
This very day—
Sweet lovers!

Sweet lovers!
Swiftly comes the noon,
And then, next thing,
The night is soon—
Fly, wing to wing.
Sweet lovers!

Sweet lovers!
Waste no single minute,
The rest of life
Has nothing in it—
Fly for your life,
Sweet lovers!

Sweet lovers!
Mark the roses yonder,
How soon they fall;

Don't plan and ponder,—
You'll lose it all,
Sweet lovers!

Sweet lovers!
Kiss you while you may;
Love, like a bird,
Soon flies away—
Ah! take my word.
Sweet lovers!

THE WOOD NYMPH

The others were all around you,
Singing and dancing there,
The wonderful night I found you
With your forest eyes and hair,
Lonely as all things fair.

Then the room and the people faded
As you turned your eyes on me,
And the woods all leafy and shaded
Grew round us tree by tree.
Safe, with no eyes to see.

And we knew we had found each other
After a thousand years;
Yea! You and I and no other,
Mated by all the spheres
A-glitter like golden tears.

And the wild-wood murmured above us,
And all the wood-land things
Came thronging there to love us,
Each little throat that sings,
And all the painted wings.

O girl, made all of wood-lilies
And starry cups of dew,
Not the mirrored moon so still is
Or wonder-hushed as you—
My moon so divinely new.

The raiment that rustled around you
Was all of young leaves made,
That wonderful night I found you
Alone in the forest-glade,
So white in the green shade.

For the room they sang and danced in.
Though the rest were unaware,
Was the wood we were entranced in,
And no one else was there—
Because we two were there.

IMMORTALITY

Dream after dream, they come and go
Face after face,
Smiting a fleeting music from the heart,
Aflame for a brief space—
How soon they pass,
Breathing a little fugitive "alas!"
But only one still keeps its ancient place,
Proudly apart,
The same brave glow
And bloom still on its face.

Face after face,
Yet still one face for me.
Year after year, spring after spring,
Snow after snow;
With magic freshness and persistency.
It will not go:
For, being gone so many an aching year,
In vain it makes pretence of vanishing
To some far sphere;
Still strangely it is here,
Never so near.

When I behold the dreams that still go on,
Still to be touched and to be gazed on still,
And see Time's writing on their weathered brows,
And mark the long endurance of old vows,
Valiantly withering;
I am most glad that face of mine is gone,
The ancient sting
Abates—yea! almost happy I grow,
Because that lovely mortal shape of her
Long since did go
Beyond the limits of my famished eyes,
Into the Paradise
Of all things fair;
And with stern Death I make my quarrel up—
For all that bitter and heart-broken cup
He to my lips one April morning set:
For now I see
It was his wizard touch upon her brow

That saves her still for me,
That, having met.
We never can part now,
She never fade, nor ever I forget.

THE EVERLASTING DOORS

I knocked at all the iron doors, crying your name,
Across the ice-bound world I sped with feet of flame,
But to my ears or to my eyes no answer came.

I stood beside the doors of spring, watching each shape
Of blue and gold that from the dark made soft escape.
Till the wide world was filled with flowers from cape to cape;

And all the doors of heaven and hell lay open wide,
And to the dead, not without hope, the living cried,
And faint and far, as in a dream, the dead replied.

Yet in that resurrection vast and rendezvous
Of parted souls that did old love renew,
I watched with wild and weary eyes in vain for you.

DESIDERIUM

There was such sweetness in the wood,
I thought you must be there,
Such wreathing and such breathing
Of blossom everywhere;
But no! it was not you, my love.
It was the rose instead,
The rose that blows and casts its snows
Above your sleeping head.

There was such laughter in the wood.
All made of you it seemed,
The singing and the ringing,
The dew that gleamed and dreamed;
Your soul sang on in every bird,
In every flower your eyes,
So blue, so true, and all so you,
Gazed out of Paradise.

Yea! all the wonder of the wood
Was you and you again,
All the flowering, and the showering
Of the bright April rain;

Yea! nought was there, however fair,
But had been you before—
Ah! for the power to turn the flower
Into the girl once more.

DREAM TRYST

She was as lovely as a flower,
And, like a flower, she passed away,
And yet, as in that morning hour
I saw her first, I still to-day
Her unforgotten face behold,
Tender as dew, and bright as gold.

Shed from her gown the old perfume,
She steals like blossom to my side,
Sweetens my thoughts, and fills the room,
And leaves me glad and sanctified;
She still about me comes and goes,
Soft as the shadow of a rose.

I know she only seemed to die,
'Tis all the happier for me
That no one sees her face but I—
So would we have it, I and she—
That no one sees us meet and part,
And hold each other heart to heart.

What trysts are ours, what moments rare,
What happy laughter side by side,
While no one dreams that she is there,
Because they think that she has died—
They'd call it dreams, were I to tell.
And so we keep our secret well.

And now it is this many a year
Since they have missed her from her place,
Healed is the wound, and dried the tear
That fell once for her vanished face;
And only I remember her,
Once so beloved and once so fair.

Once!— ah! beloved, if they could know!
If they as I could see you still,
And watch your beauty lovelier grow,
And feast their eyes and drink their fill
Of all that breath and bloom of you—
Ah! I might lose you, if they knew.

But now no eyes but mine can see.
No hands can touch, no ears can hear,
And none can come 'twixt you and me,
No other lover hold you dear;
And Time that other beauty mars
Can reach you not among the stars.

SILENCIEUX

Always it was the same—always the same;
I called—she heeded not; my heart ached on;
Then to my side, without a word, she came,
Sat with me, and, without a word, was gone:
All my poor supplication was in vain,
And my life stopped until she came again.

Once, a whole summer day beneath the trees,
I drank her beauty with my famished eyes,
My head at peace upon her quiet knees;
The rustle of her gown was Paradise:
An altar stands for ever in the place
Where once all day I looked into her face.

And then a year went by, nor sight, nor word,
Had I to live on whose whole life was she,
Till, like the sudden singing of a bird
Once more she came, and stood and smiled on me,
And took a little pity on my drouth.
Lifting to me the mercy of her mouth.

One night she came—the stars were in her hair—
She took my head, and kissed it into rest,
And then the moon rose, white and unaware,
The moon—or did I dream it was her breast?
I think no moon that ever walked the night,
Nor any lily, was ever half so white.

Then came a hush of days like none before,
A distance echoing and full of dread
That seemed to tell me she would come no more,
A frozen whisper saying she was dead;
Yet i, whose life she is, and so well knew
Her silent ways, would not believe it true.

Nor will I yet—for ever was it so,
Silent so long —so long—would she remain.
Then like a spirit softly come and go:
So, on a sudden, shall she come again,
Step, silver-footed, out of the still air,

Finger on lip—for me to follow her.

TILL WE FORGET

If all we love and all we dream
Must on the wind be swept away,
And all that's brave and all that's fair
Be lost like music on the air.
Like blossoms on a running stream,
And all our wealth be Yesterday—
Still would I love, still would I dream.

What though the kiss that once she gave
Be hidden with her in the grave,
What though the life she once did bless
Withers with a great weariness,
What though not any hope have I
Once more to see her when I die,
Her hallowed lips, one summer day,
Made the green world to fade away—
That glory burns about me yet,
It cannot go—till I forget.

Not to forget! Life's art is there:
To vanished faces keep our word,
Thus brighter grow they, year by year.
Nearer they come, and clearlier heard
The voices that we used to hear—
Eyes of the dead, how soft ye shine!—
Nor can that beauty ever fade
Which passed into the magic shade
Where Memory dreams above her shrine.

Enough it is if we can hold
Still in our hands our ancient gold—
Gold of great hours that could not last,
Yet last for ever—holden fast
By faith of heart that needs no more
Or better than it had before,
And deems the Past the Present yet,
That cannot fade—till we forget.

WHEN I GO WALKING IN THE WOODS

When I go walking in the woods,
I take one thought with me,
And, unaware,

I find it there
Beside me in the sea;
Yea! could I fly,
I doubt not I
Would find it in the air:
Companion of all solitudes,
It is the thought of her.

And, when I fall asleep at night.
But for one thing I pray:
The power that stole
Away her soul
To bring it back some day;
And all my dreams,
Till morning gleams,
That through the day console,
Smell sweet of her, with her are bright,
As with an aureole.

And, sometimes in the afternoon,
When all is strange and still,
When sunshine sleeps
In the sea's deeps,
And loiters on the hill,
I seem to hear
A footstep near,
A sound of one who creeps
Softly, to listen—then, too soon,
The sound of one who weeps.

VIOLIN MUSIC

Somewhere to-night among the hills of heaven
She walks, with all her stars around her;
And I who lost her here on earth
Grow happy, knowing God has found her.

So many days along all paths of radiance
Made for her feet to tread I sought her,
Through all the wide lagoons of dawn
And mazy lanes of moonlit water.

Now know I by the path of this strange music
Beyond the world she went a-straying,
Almost you bring me where she walks—
Ah! for the love of God, cease not your playing.

Long had the far sea lured me
And the eyes of the waste,
But I said: "I must stay in the town
With my beautiful face,
Earning our bread together—
Ah! sweet to the taste
As honey, wild honey, dropping the rocks a-down,
And kisses for every weather."

But now that no more, each morning,
We look in each other's eyes,
Poor as our attic sparrows,
But happy as Paradise—
And she in her simple adorning
The Queen of the Islands of Spice;
What more is the town to me
That I like a ghost should linger?
So again comes the song of the sea,
That luring and lordliest singer,
And again shine the eyes of the waste.
And they say: "You shall find her no more,
For all the long nights you have paced,
Street after street, through the town,
Street after street;
Vainly you knock at each door,
Vainly pray for the sound of her feet,
For the tender talk of her gown—
For she dwells no more in the town."

So I think I shall go far away,
To the sky-line's loneliest ends,
Where the ships leave the men every day
That have no more need of friends,
Nothing more to do or to say;
Where the sky and the sea are alone
For ever, year after year,
And the near is one with the far,
And the far with the near.
And perhaps in some sea-sung place,
Where the sands are as white as her breast,
I shall see, or dream that I see,
Once more my beautiful face;
And think it is I and she
In the town once more together,
With kisses for every weather;
Our bread to earn for the day,
And earning for night our rest.

And so I am going away

Where the sands are as white as her breast.

TIME

As the days go, and as some plan
'Mid all my wanderings I discern,
Divinely hid when I began
This curious pilgrimage of man,—
Knowing it all, yet all to learn!—
With plumed feet on the flaming quest,
I come to see that Time knew best.

The loss that smote my heart in twain.
The bitterness of young despair,
The face I shall not see again:
Glad grow I of that ancient pain;
Fair though that face, and still how fair!
I do not sorrow any more—
Time kept a fairer face in store.

Not to have lost were loss indeed!
I smile back on the frantic boy,
Alight with hope, and flushed with speed,
Who could not know his spirit freed,
As, one by one. Time took each joy,
Each cherished bauble of desire,
And sternly cast them on the fire.

Thus, eased of things of no avail,
Wishes that burden, dreams that die,
My light boat spreads a fearless sail,
Laughing alike with sun and gale.
Safe as a bird is in the sky—
Her cargo now is nought but gold;
Her port—I have not yet been told.

THE ROSE SING I

The Rose sing I—yet not for me she grows;
I sing the Vine—yet all untasted goes
The golden cup intoxicant with fire:
Be thou my Vine, and O be thou my Rose.

V

She was a little girl who loved the town.
She had no thought in the world
But to kiss and drown;
Joy was she all through and through,
Wild as a bird was she,
As a wild rose filled with dew;
Work liked she not, nor had she wish to do
Aught but to laugh and love right merrily,
And watch the bubbles rising in the glass—
Our little Mary—sweet little Mary—
Alack! and alas!

It was as though she were made but of eyes and hair,
And a red red mouth;
No thought had she in her sweet small head,
Books read she not—^she kissed instead,
Like a desert aflame with drouth;
For, though of kisses she drained a thousand score,
She would laugh unappeased and cry out for more;
She counted neither kisses nor the cost.
She was very young, and some who loved her well
Said "Mary will be lost—
Our little Mary will go down into deep hell,
Unless we send her back to the country and the grass;
For there are many hawks in the town," said they,
"For little birds like you, Mary, you must not stay;
You must go back and be safe with good country folk,
And say your prayers again and bear the yoke,
And be a good girl, Mary,"—and Mary went
Home very sad and obedient.
And I, for one,
Am very sorry for Mary, and wish she had not gone.

For I know right well
That, being as God made her, caring nought for birds
Or flocks or herds,
Humdrum work of the house,
Pigs and chickens and cows,
The country will help her not with its stars and flowers,
She will be Mary there as she was Mary here;
She will still be ours,
That love as she loved them the shining streets
At midnight more than the Milky Way,
And stolen joys and forbidden sweets;
And I dare to say
She had been safer here with us in the town,
Than by running streams or on daisied down.
For, as birds are born for the air and fish for the sea,
She was not born to be good as good people be,

Not born for dulness and duty, but only glee;
And we who can drink the cup with a steady hand
Had taught our little Mary the way to be wise
Even in folly, brought her to understand
The half is more than the whole,
And saved her innocent eyes,
And saved her soul.

But now for Mary a great fear have I:
There in the country, with the pigs and cows
And family Bibles, she shall fret and sigh,
And all her prisoned thoughts dream and carouse
In pleasures lost—till on a sudden day
Mary shall up and out and far away
Back to the town,
And seize the cup once more, and drain it down
And kiss . . . and this time drown.

FROM GENERATION TO GENERATION

Never a lovelier lady
Hallowed the eyes of men.
It hardly seems that Nature
Can make such a face again;
She walked like the early morning
Over the meadows of dew—
Was there ever a lovelier lady?"
And the three of us sighed "It is true."

And we talked of her sorrowful going,
And the blank she had left behind,
And the ways of the wind past knowing,
And the lost that we never find.
Then lo! as we spoke to each other
There passed by the open door,
Lovely as Eros' mother,
A girl none had seen before;

And we sprang from our lonely talking,
And gazed with regretful eyes
On the marvellous way of her walking—
Sad men that can never be wise!—
While she passed in her insolent glory,
With never a look behind!
And again we sat down to our story
Of the fairness of womankind.

Then one of us said: "I am thinking
That when twenty years have gone by,

Some men will be sitting drinking.
And dreaming as you and I
Of that girl and her wonderful walking
That went but now by the door—
And the burden of all their talking:
'There are faces like that no more.'"

THE IDOL

Dear lad, let go her eyes.
They seem so blue,
So young and true;
Yet, if you only knew,
Could you be wise!
If you could only see
Her half as dear as she
Sees you!
And all this ivory,
And all this gold,
O is it possible
You have not been told
How often, how often,
They were bought and sold;
What hands have dared
To touch this ivory,
What vulgar fingers
Wandered in this gold!

Dear lad, had you but heard
From those red lips—
One strange dishevelled word,
How white your own soul would have seemed to you!
Then had you known
What sits upon the throne
Made by your pure heart and adoring knee;
That not in her
But you the worshipper
The wonder lives and all the mystery;
That but a mound of scented dust
Is she,
Shaped by your dreaming eyes
That cannot see,
A lamia of lust
In mask of Paradise,
A withered foulness, a stale harlotry!

You are not half so lovely as you deem,
I know a thousand things that are more fair—
Poor child, whose looking-glass is all your dream,
Holding the worshipped and the worshipper
Tranced in a sort of visual embrace.
No eyes will ever look into your eyes
As your own face looks into your own face,
Fair though it be—its fairness none denies;
No lover's knee will bend so long or low
As you bend to this image that is you:
Have you not heard of faces long ago,—
Helen's and Iseult's—that were lovely too?
And have you thought that, when your face is gone.
Lost like a faded garment too long worn,
A shrouded thing the dust and moths devour,
Of all the beauty men shall look upon,
Those golden faces that are yet unborn.
Waiting like buds upon the earth to flower?

But, even as now your face you dote upon,
I think of many fairer things there are;
I will not crush you with comparison
Of the young moon or of the morning star,
Nor even will I match you with the rose—
What woman yet was ever fair as those?

But I will take this shell into my hand,
Ponder its shape in faery oceans wrought,
Lonely and perfect, where the coral sand
Spreads its white floor, and the sea sighs its thought.
I know a fish within that turquoise sea
That I had rather look on all the day—
Mailed like a knight, yet like a flower is he—
Yes! I would rather sit and watch him sway.
With crusted jewels for his foolish eyes,
Poised in that liquid lapis-lazuli,
Than kiss the fairest woman 'neath the skies.

I know a snake that glides among the rocks,—
Not Aphrodite naked in the spray,
Nor Aphrodite with a thousand frocks,
Knows such a spell to steal my wits away.
I know a beetle made of bronze and blue,
With dusty gold about his armoured thighs,—
Can you believe him lovelier than you?
And shall I tell you of my butterflies?

Nay! I will cease, I would not bring the frown
That writes the wrinkle; I too much adore
The face, Narcissa, that—you love still more.

A butterfly might wear that evening gown,
To-night my beetle pales, my fish grows dim,
My snake—yea! I grow faithless even to him.
But, dear, if in your glass you once could smile,
Happy in your own beauty, yet knowing too—
There are a thousand things more fair than you,
And beauty is but for a little while.

LITTLE LADY ECHO

She is such a pretty child,
With her wistful delicate ways,
Her veiled mock-mystic eyes,
And her mimicking art of praise,
Her lisping, silvery, lies;
Saying over and over,
Like some daft and dreaming lover,
Our idlest phrase;
Ah! how one wearies, all unbeguiled.
Of the duplicate things she says.

TO A YOUNG GIRL

Dare not tell a creature young as thou.
Thou innocent unfolding miracle
'Twixt girl and woman; 'tis too early now
For thee, and soon for me too late, to tell.

In thee I sight another's promised land
That with another's milk and honey flows;
Alas! not mine is the predestined hand
That shall stretch forth some day and take thy rose.

Only its shadow in the morning sun
Falls on the westering path my feet must take;
Of all thy petals, not for pity's sake
Will thy rose-gatherer spare a single one.

All will he have—yea! all thy sweetness hoard,
Miser of thee, though starved go all the rest;
Stern keeper of the garden of thy breast,
Of all thy treasure absolute dread lord.

May he be good to thee, thou little flower
That in the morning hath so sweet a smell;
If he should only wear thee for an hour—
Then shall I wish that I had dared to tell.

TO A BOY, ON THE DEATH OF HIS SWEET-HEART

You say she died last night, and was so fair—
Come, let us sit and talk, and tell me all—
But twenty was she, and such golden hair!
And O to-morrow is her funeral. . . .

Your life goes with her—you are twenty-two?—
Come, drink this glass, and tell me more of her—
Her hair was gold, you said, her eyes were blue;
She was too young to die, she was too fair.

And all the treasure of her heart and mind
Rifled and wasted, lost and gone—ah! where?
And all her beauty scattered on the wind,
Like rose-leaves on the garden here and there.

And nought is left for you except to die,
Or be her pilgrim, till you meet once more;
Hers was the loveliest face under the sky,
Time never made a face like hers before.

Ah! let me go with you, and kneel and pray,
And take these flowers, sweet as her young breath;
And then, at the sad ending of the day,
Let you and I for her give thanks to Death—

Death that was kind and loved her all too well
To watch her beauty wither here away,
But took her while she had so sweet a smell,
All in her blossom, like a hawthorn spray.

Death that was kind to her is kind to you:
Though eighty years shall whiten on your head,
She still shall be the morning and the dew,
And live for ever lovely, being dead.

IF I WERE RICH, LITTLE GIRL

If I were rich, little girl, little girl,
I'd build you a castle all of pearl,
With towers that touched the tip of the moon;
Girded about with a sea-like tune
Of forests black with the star-kissed pine;
And I should be yours and you should be mine
For ever and ever, week in—week out;

And in the forests beasts should range,
Unicorns
With gilded horns,
And other monsters fierce and strange,
To keep the vulgar out.

And we should ponder all the day
On the blue lotus in the moat,
Or hear the hidden minstrels play
On strings of gold;
Or some slim lad with honeyed throat
Should sing and say,
After the old Provenfal way,
Our love that never can grow old;
Or in the scutcheoned chapel pray—
If I were rich; ah! well-a-day.

And, when the evening star began
To trim its silver lamp on high,
Beloved of God, forgot of man,
Up many a happy winding stair,
We'd laughing run,
And watch the sinking of the sun,
And the wide meadows of the air
Filling with flowers—
And kiss and turn away and sigh;
Till east and west and north and south
Were nought but darkness and your mouth—
While eagles on the topmost towers
Guarded us from the sky.

If I were rich, little girl,—said I.

LE ROI FAINÉANT

I was born idle, and meant for summer days,
Where the sea is ever blue
And the palm for ever sways,—
O how I hate winter and all his ways!

I was born idle to sit upon a throne,
With a queen for ever You,
Like a lily scarcely blown.
With your eyes carved out of a big moonstone.

I was born idle to dream my life away,
With a young moon ever new,
And the world for ever May,
And the sound of streams in my ears alway.

I was born idle to lie at last in state,
While the royal trumpets blew
O'er a royal head too great
For a world so small—and so second-rate.

ANSWER TO AN INVITATION

Yes! I will play, but it must be with fire,
Though only for an hour should be the game—
I care not if I burn, so you be flame;
But bring me not the small change of desire.

Yes! I will sail, if you fear not to drown,
If you fear not to swim the unfathomed sea,
To dive into its moonlit heart with me,
Hand in my hand, down deep, and still deep down.

Yes! I will fly, if you fear not the height,
Nor yet the depth, of all that blue abyss,—
Love spans it in the lightning of a kiss—
For you and me be there no lesser flight.

I will not make a toy of this strange thing
That, at your touch, goes calling through my veins,
The god each petty amorist profanes—
Your little kisses to the winds I fling.

Nor of your beauty will I honey take,
Sipping and tasting of you like a bee;
Let other smaller folk their small love make—
'Tis a far other love for you and me.

But if you come to me with wild lost lips,
In a great darkness made of a great light,
Then shall our wings mount in an equal flight,
Nor fear, though all the firmament eclipse.

Though from the zenith to the pit we fall,
Breast against breast, and eyes adream on eyes,
We shall be one with suns and seas and skies—
The power and the glory of it all.

LOVE'S PHILOSOPHY

Ah! Sweetheart, seek not to explain
Why grass is green and skies are blue,

Nor mar, with small enquiring brain,
What wiser heads than I and you
Pondered, yet fathomed not—'tis best
To marvel, and to leave the rest.

To worship, not to comprehend,
You are as lovely as you are;
And so it is, enchanted friend,
With water-lily and with star;
And—Love, what means it? Ask as soon
The meaning of the rising moon.

O is it not enough to draw
This breath of being, you and I,
Girt round with loveliness and awe?
Why should we ask the reason why?
The gods gave us this summer day
To love in—not explain why

O lips as red as yonder rose,
I kiss and question not—content;
Nor spoil such poesy with prose
Of what the high immortals meant—
To pack with such mysterious bliss
The simple action of a kiss.

Nor why this fury of delight,
Blent so with pathos and with pain.
Ah! love, too soon draws on the night,
Kiss—lest we never kiss again!
I cannot tell the reason why.
But I shall love you till I die.

THE SHADOW OF KNOWLEDGE

I am too sad with knowledge not to know
A dream is but a dream:
So many faces covered up with snow,
That had so brave a gleam,
Have gone with wind and stream.

They might not stay for all their valiance;
Nor shall this face I hold,
Praying to keep it mine 'gainst Time and Chance,
Flooding my heart with gold,
Escape, even it, the cold.

Even as this summer day so hot and sweet,
So deep in flowers and grass.

This marble that is you from head to feet.
Like some frail bloom, shall pass.
Or shadow in a glass.

In vain with desperate eyes I drink your eyes,
In vain with desperate hands
Fold you and love you; and, with desperate lies,
Would cheat the running sands—
Alas! Love understands.

Yea! and Love understands a wiser thing
Even than Wisdom knows:
That Joy is Joy, albeit so swift of wing,
And, though so soon it goes,
The Rose—ah! 'tis the Rose.

AT MIDSUMMER

Do you remember how we used to go
Into the woods at midsummer?—
For, after all, 'twas not so long ago—
And leave our horses tethered by the stream.
And then steal farther in to kiss and dream—
At midsummer.

A hidden place it was of rock and pine.
There would we eat our bread and drink our wine.
And laugh—ah! how we laughed the laugh divine,
There in the woods at midsummer.

Then on a sudden grave and strange we were.
With joy, like anguish, holding fast our eyes.
While I would frame your face in your deep hair
Falling across the hills of Paradise;
And start, for fear 'twas foot of some chance comer,
There in the woods at midsummer.

The blossoms of the year had ceased to blow,
Just a green palace shorn of ornament
The July woods, and surely long ago
Melted the last hid snow, sans argument;
Yet I found both the blossoms and the snow,
There in the woods at midsummer.

THE WIND'S WAY

The winds of the world for a little season

Blew us together heart to heart,
But now, alas! with the wind's unreason,
The winds of the world must blow us apart.

And thou to the north, and I to the south,
Must wander away into loveless lands,
With a last long anguish of mouth on mouth,
And a last despair of dissevered hands.

O winds of the world that blew us together.
Winds of the world that blow us apart,
Will it ever again be lovers' weather,
Shall we ever again be heart to heart?

VI

THE ETERNAL PLAY

(To Robert H. Davis)

Third act of the eternal play!
In poster-like emblazonries,
"Autumn once more begins to-day"—
'Tis written all across the trees
In yellow letters like Chinese.

A classic of the antique school,
Of which 'twere all in vain to tire,
Writ to inexorable rule,
And fed with stern dramatic fire—
Ah! Demiurgus of the lyre.

Lovely as stern the art that wields
The rock, the rainbow, and the rose,
Scatters blue flowers along the fields,
Alike the bolt of thunder throws,
And from its hand lets fall the snows.

How many hundred centuries
Hath run this play, with ne'er a pause!
That which this living audience sees
Thrilled all the dead to wild applause—
And yet the strange old drama draws.

No need to change the piece a whit—
The audience changes all the time;
New millions crowd to witness it,
Each hour the clock beats out a chime:
This ancient masterpiece of rhyme.

For never rhyme was like to this,
Since star matched star across the deep,
Or sound with sound first learned to kiss,
And Time was given this rhythm to keep
Of song and sunshine, dreams and sleep.

Not all alike adjudge the play:
Some laugh, some weep, and some there be
Deem the old classics's had its day,
And some scarce any of it see,
Nodding in witless apathy.

And Others more than all the rest
One act out of the four prefer—
Spring, in her wind-flower draperies drest,
Or Summer, with her bosom bare;
Winter than these some deem more fair.

Some, mayhap melancholic, deem
Autumn the meaning of the play—
The smile that says, "Twas all a dream!"
The sigh that says, "I can but stay
A little while, and then away";

The rustling robe of joy that ends,
The moon-cold kiss upon the brow,
The fading sail of sea-sped friends,
The love that is another's now,
The voice that mourns, "Ah! where art thou?"

For all her purple and her gold,
Autumn hath such a tale to tell—
The tale that tells us all is told;
Yea! but she tells it wondrous well.
Weaving strange hope into her spell:

The hope that, when we sit no more
At this old play, and needs must go
Through yonder shrouded exit door,
The mystic impresario
Hath still for us a stranger show.

TO THE SKUNK CABBAGE

Will no one sing thee? Then will I.
The violet, though herself should die,
Hath songs to keep her living still;
The laureates of the daffodil

Fill half the painted books of song;
And, all the perfumed summer long,
For every magic hour she blows,
A thousand minstrels hath the rose.

Ah! what a pampered state is theirs,
Nursed by soft rains and April airs,
Spoiled darlings of the earth and sky;
Whilst thou in fetid swamps must lie,
Outcast from kindness, as from fame,
Banned by an evil-smelling name.

Yet, who, as thou, when all is drear,
The dark beginning of the year,
Lifts up so brave a torch on high,
In boggy woodlands black with mire,
Leaping with sudden urns of fire—

The only brightness in the world?
And not another leaf uncurled
In all the landscape far or near—
Of all the glories of the year
The mocked resplendent pioneer.

THE SNOWDROP

The snow and the rain are falling together,
And there on my window-pane
The frost makes pictures out of my sighs—
As I watch for those everlasting eyes
That I shall not see again,
April or winter weather.

Yet the snowdrop whispers under the snow:
"I too am dwelling beneath the ground,
But in spring you shall see me blow,
Like a long-lost jewel found;
And your two bright sleeping eyes
Shall wake as they were before,
And your long-lost face shall rise
Through the soft green grave-yard floor.
There is much music underground,"
Said the snowdrop under the snow.

DOGWOOD

If Earth had nothing else to speak for her,

Her only lovely vindication thou,
Thou in a cindered waste the sole thing fair,
Framed in the dross and basalt of despair,
But only thy dew-drenched siderial bough
A lonely witchcraft there.

If the great sea were not, with all its blue,
And forests with green continents of dew;
If all were wilderness, and brutish things,
Travail of wallowing slime and shuddering stone,
No plumage gay and happy flight of wings,
But only thou alone—
There 'mid fanged horror and abysmal storm,
And boiling floods and drift of flaming sleet;
Annunciation magically sweet,
Thy frail triumphant form,
A lovely spectre from the dark up-sent,
Radiantly innocent;
It were enough assurance that some soul
Of starry purpose through the blindness moved,
And, 'mid the hard-wrung travail of the whole,
That something dreamed and loved.

One spray of dogwood, though the rest were hell,
Were faith enough, enough of miracle,
The heart and end of being to foretell.
Eyes that in spring have seen the dogwood shine
Need ask from earth no other seal or sign,
Nor fear at last within that mould to lie
That lifts such fairness from the darkling deep,
Perfect against the singing April sky—
Nor shrink in such a bed to fall asleep.

LADY APRIL

So, April, here thou art again,
Thou pretty pretty lady!
With broidered skirts of sun-kissed rain—
A grown-up girl already!
Thy sister May
Is on her way,
And June, with tresses shady;
But, of the three,
I love best thee—
Thou pretty pretty lady!

Thou hauntest all the sobering year,
With echoes of thy laughter;
And life is nought till thou appear,

And but remembrance after.
Though Autumn's yield
From garth and field
Run o'er from floor to rafter,
Thy wild-rose breast
Haunts all the rest,
And makes it poor with laughter.

WOOD FLOWER

I found a flower in the wood,
Growing softly by some water;
Had I plucked it when I could,
The old wild-wood's fairy daughter—
Not thus vainly had I sought her.

So deep a spell was on me laid,
I might not stretch my hand to take her,
So fragile she, I was afraid
Even my lightest touch would break her—
And now, alas, what voice shall wake her!

THE LITTLE RILLS

The little rills
That from the hills
Come trickling down to feed the river.
That sing unheard
Save by poet and bird—
Each little giver
To the great river.

The Seine and the Thames
Have lordly fames,
And the Rhine and the Po
'Neath laurels flow;
But the little streams,
With their whispered dreams,
May sing forever,
And no one know.

Would I could make
A song for their sake!
But I myself go singing unheard,
Save once in a while by poet and bird.

SWEETHEART APRIL

Immortal sweetheart of the year,
April, old Winter's darling;
The young frogs in the reedy mere.
Long before I, knew you were here;
So did the starling.

The old wood knew it long ago.
For he had felt you stealing,
To press your lips beneath the snow
Where the arbutus creeps to blow.
Shyly concealing.

Still prisoned, too, the ice-hung stream.
With half-heard laughing water,
Sang low of you, as in a dream,
To every Wandering breeze and beam,—
Earth's dazzling daughter,

That now, like some young maenad flings
Her flaming heart on gladness,
Yet hath in all the songs she sings,
'Mid all the wildness and the wings,
The ache of sadness.

Sing to a younger heart than mine,
Sweet April! promise-maker,
Dear sorceress of shower and shine,
Duping us still with dreams divine,
O April, promise-breaker!

A SUMMER DAY

Work? Not to-day! Ah! no—that were to do
The gracious face of heaven a surly wrong,
Bright day so manifestly made for song,
And sweep of freedom's wings into the blue.
Divinely idle, rather let us lie.
And watch the lordly unindustrious sky.
Nor trail the smoke of little busy cares
Across its calm—Work? Not to-day! not I!

Work? Why, another year . . . one never knows
But this the flowering last of all our years;
Which of us can be sure of next year's rose?
And I, that have so loved them all my days,
Not yet have learned the names of half the flowers,

Nor half enough have listened to the birds.

Nay! while the marvel of the May is ours,
Earth's book of lovely hieroglyphic words
Let's read together, each green letter spell.
And each illuminated miracle,
Decking the mystic text with blue and gold—
That Book of Beauty where all Truth is told.

Let's watch the dogwood, holding silver trays
Of blossom out across the woodland ways,
Whiter than breast of any mortal girl's;
And hark! yon bird flinging its song like pearls,
Sad as all lovely things fore-doomed to die—
Work? Not to-day! Ah! no—not you, not I.

TO A MOUNTAIN BROOK

You could not sing, nor yet could I,
If all your path ran smooth as glass,
A moving mirror of the sky,
In a long frame of quiet grass,
With fleur-de-lis and arrow-head.
To grace you as you pass:
You need rough pebbles for your bed,
And the ledged rock to make you strong,
Hurling you down from height to height
In frenzied leaps of panic white,—
To make you fierce for song;
Boulders that dance you round and round
With guttural jollities of sound,
And gullies grim,
And caverns dim,
And floors of shale, and walls of slate;
And many a time to lose your way,
'Mid snag and snarl and scummed morass,
Making a dolorous delay
In your bright wayward travelling—
Nothing to do but brim and wait,
Till, like the opening of a gate,
The valley comes, and down you fling,
Knowing so many songs to sing,
So many warbling ways of rhyme,
Kissed sweet again with mint and thyme,
Full throated with a thousand springs—
A singing victor, proud and strong,
That made of rocks his vowelled song.

THE SECRET OF THE WOODS

The secret of the woods lies close,
Behind a thousand leafy doors;
The mountain laurel and the rose
Make fair the winding corridors
Through which my frequent footstep goes
Along the velvet mossy floors;
The rustling arras swings aside,
And swings behind me, as I fare;
But still the woods their secret hide.
Yet is it whispered everywhere.
And every creature there, save I,
Knows it by heart: the bee could tell.
Had it a mind; the butterfly
Floats with it painted on its wings;
Even the woodchuck knows it well,
And nothing else the cat-bird sings.
Would I were as these soul-less things,
These beings of the element,
Soul-less, yet all of spirit blent.
Wild essences of fire and dew—
Then had mine ears been more attent,
And I had known the secret too.

THE LAST SONG OF THE NIGHTINGALE TO THE ROSE

Ere thou must fade, and I must go
Along the pathway of the snow.
Divine companion, whom to praise
I sang my secret roundelays
Through all the golden nights of June,
While stole the young eavesdropping moon
To listen, and the night stood still
To make a silence for my song;
O Marvel, ere thy petals spill
Upon the garden grass, my tongue
To sing thee to thy sleep is fain—
Till, as of old, thou comest again.

So many ages thou and I
Have bloomed and sung and seemed to die,
Losing to find, finding to lose,—
Thou chalice of enchanted dews.
Thou being born of the soft breath
Of Beauty through a thousand springs,
With bosom bared, flaunting at death;
Thou little shape that gathers up

All colour in one magic cup,
And to the eye a glory brings
Past the magnificence of kings.

Since I was bird, and thou wert rose,
Constant across the gulfs of Time,
Even as a poet shapes his rhyme
Till with a perfect art it goes,
So I thy beauty strove to sing
In music lordlier each Spring—
Yet shall my song forever be
But as a shadow cast by thee.

I go into the dark, as thou—
For lo! the red leaf on the bough
Signals the passage and decay
Of Beauty's transitory day;
Yet shall I ponder, as we lie
Far from the summer-scented sky,
Nearer to thee in song to climb,
When I, with sure resurgent Time,
At twilight, in some garden close,
Am bird once more, and thou a rose.

SEPTEMBER

I that loved Spring am Autumn's lover now,
Impatient for the passing of the rose,
And glad, I scarce know why, that Summer goes,
With all her noisy splendours—ah! but thou,
Grey-eyed September, thee do I avow
My mistress, till the last effacing snows—
Thou passion that hast learned a queen's repose,
I bring thee Youth grown Wisdom, Time knows how.

For in thine heart, as in thy haunted eyes,
Memory and youth in one enchantment blend,
And, still more wonderful than thou art wise,
Though fair as April—how much more a friend!
Not for the lips of an unlearned boy
Is mingled thy strange cup of fearful joy.

AUTUMN

The autumn tints! ah! yes, I know—
The glories of the afterglow!
But who would give one day of spring

For this fantastic motley thing?

This tapestry is woven fair
With yellow leaves and leaves blood-red—
So on an Eastern sepulchre
The gaudy patterned rugs are spread;
This painted woodland—be it said—
Bannered and blazoned with decay,
Is like a minster, where the dead
Lie laurelled, waiting Judgment Day,
In scutcheoned vault and sculptured urn,
With withered garlands dryly decked;
In vain some random glories burn,
Where all is woe-begone and wrecked.

'Tis but a waving arras screen,
Moved by the sad autumnal wind,
Hiding, like some theatric scene,
The final change that lurks behind.
'Tis but a vaunt of doomed things:
The golden-rod all vainly blows,
And, purple as the pall of kings,
The aster vainly apes the rose.

So spake I, dreary as the rain,
Sobbing against the window pane,
Sad as the wind that at my door
Went crying "Never—Nevermore."

LA CIGALE

(For J. R.)

I found him limping in the grass—
Poor little shivering fellow!
He had not many days, alas!
For all the leaves were yellow.

I took him in beside the stove,
And fed him beads of honey,
And brought a brother-singer's love—
He never asked for money.

And soon he gave a chirp or two,
And seemed quite brave and jolly;
And, as he sipped his golden brew,
Sang—"Down with melancholy!"

THE GARDEN GOD

My garden prospers not, unless I bring
To the old garden god his offering,
Each day at dawn, and then at eve again;
In vain I water, and I weed in vain,
Am vainly suppliant to the sullen seed,
Unless the god of gardens intercede.

Far down the flickering orchard is his shrine,
With canopy of every wandering vine
Roofed in; and rippling poplars, all day long,
Bring him their delicately whispered song;
While, in his leafy chancel comes and goes
Incense of honeysuckle and wild rose;
And the great candles of his altar are,
Each day, the morning and the evening star.

The thrush and blackbird are his choristers,
And in his keeping all the little cares
Of little lives, and little frightened prayers,
To him the firstlings of the flowering spring
I, with a heart devout and jocund, bring:
The infant snowdrop that the winter dares.
The crocus that in sudden flame up-rears.
The first shy violet, the first daffodil,
Blowing his yellow trumpet on the hill;
Cherry and apple bloom in hand bring I,
And fairy almond boughs so quick to die.

Then, when the fury of the spring is spent,
And bloom on fruit and berry is intent,
The first red apple sweetening on the bough
I bring, with happy heart and pious vow.
And, all the summer and the autumn through,
First flowers and fruits 1 bring, in order due,
Till, with the yellow and the crimson leaves,
The purple grapes are come and golden sheaves.
Then 1 with ears of corn bedeck the shrine,
And globed clusters of the gladdening vine;
And, when the year grows to its sorrowing close,
Nor on the earth is left a single rose,
But the sad aster and the golden-rod
Over the dying landscape dream and nod,
For his last garland weave I even these,
'Mid thinning bowers and sighing memories;
Till the first snow-flakes come a-fluttering down
And make of their cold flowers his winter crown.

PAN

Ye that have deemed of Pan as shepherds sing,
With soft pipe fluting in some leafy dale,
Know of the earthquake too is he the king,
And where the violet-sloped volcanoes fling
Their lovely unloved streams into the vale.

Dear to his heart, no less than gentle rills
Touching the whispering music from the reeds,
The rainbowed lava flooding through the hills,
Fairer by every faery thing it kills,
And decked with flowers no poet plucks or heeds.

Yea! of the winter, too, is he the lord,
And for his pleasaunce and his mansion takes
The pinnacled ice of polar wastes abhorred.
Even as some brambled bower on a green sward;
Alike the windflower and the mountain shakes,

Hearing his tread; and, as some iron string.
No less the pines vibrate than each soft dome
Chimes in a maiden's breast when he doth sing—
For from the lips of this rock-hearted king
Falls sweetness as of honey from the comb.

SEA-SORCERY

Did you ever feel this about the sea.
In her huge enfolding ecstasy
Lost as you lay,
Adream and asway—
That you yourself were about to be
Rock and sea-weed, and even as she?
That you swayed and swung on the brink of a change,
A wordless glory, a wild and strange
Translation blindingly swift and sweet;
That, a moment more,
And a secret door,
As it were, would open and take you in,
And you and the sea be kin and kin,
And the land nevermore be pressed of your feet.

Ah! when your heart is filled full with the sea,
And your body hangs poised, like a crystal sphere,
In an infinite ether of mystical glee,
Streamed through and through,
Like the sunlit dew,

With a glory of gold,
And a glory of blue;
With the delicate vastness of heaven as near
And soft as a flower or a tear;
Flesh no more, but a thing to hold
Joy like a cup and song like a bird:
Only in music is hidden the word
For the height and the depth of your ecstasy,
Lost in a palace of light, and alone,
As a god is alone, with the sea.

O then of the sea have a care!
In that moment of high content
Is the mystical snare;
It was that the wise Greek meant
By the sea-nymph and her hair.
Call back your heart, lest it fill
Too full of felicity,
Your mortal heart, lest it break
With too much of divinity,
And the soul of waters enter in,
And you and the sea be kin and kin!
Ah! then shall you watch, as she sways and sings,
The earth and its folk as alien things.

ELEMENTAL COMRADES

When you are sad, always remember this—
The sea is blue forever,
And nothing in the sky can go amiss;
The promise of the stars was broken never.
Always the tide is punctual to the weed,
And to the little barnacle that waits,
Sighing for love of it in its great need.
Yea, great and small miraculously are mates,
Calling and answering one unto the other:
Why, therefore, sad? Something on sea or land
Your lovely sister is, or your brave brother,
Waiting mysteriously to take your hand.
Thus, understanding that all things that are—
Volcanoes and the yellow butterfly.
The coral climbing to the evening star—
Are one together, shall not you and I
Be brave from all this wonder, and have faith
That colour is man's comrade, and those forms
Meaningless save for beauty that nothing saith?
And know, long since, man was the friend of storms.

SAILING

Blue sea and white sail
All day together,
From moon-set to moon-rise,
Not a sign of weather!
Hid like some deep-sea pearl,
Deep in the heart a girl—
Like the sea singing.

Foaming sea-laces—
Ah! for her breast,
Ever a-stirring.
Ever at rest;
Far-off sea-spaces
Meeting the skies,
All the world's distance
Dwells in her eyes,
All the world's sorrow
At the heart lies—
Like the sea sighing.

MORNING AT SEA

Out of the constant east the breeze
Brings morning, like a wafted rose,
Across the glimmering lagoon,
And wakes the still palmetto trees.
And blows adrift the phantom moon.
That paler and still paler glows—

Up with the anchor—let's be going!
O hoist the sail—and let's be going!
Glory and glee
Of the morning sea—
Ah! let's be going.

Under our keel, a glass of dreams.
Still fairer than the morning sky,
A jewel shot with blue and gold,
The swaying clearness streams and gleams;
A crystal mountain smoothly rolled
O'er magic gardens flowing by
Over we go the sea-fans waving.
Over the rainbow corals paving
The deep-sea floor;
No more, no more,
Would I seek the shore

To make my grave in—
O sea-fans waving.

CORAL ISLES AND TROPIC SEAS

The dotted cays,
With their little trees,
Lie all about on the crystal floor;
Nothing but beauty—
Far off is duty,
Far off the folk of the busy shore.

The mangroves stride
In the coloured tide,
With leafy crests that will soon be isles;
And all is lonely—
White sea sand only,
Angel-pure for untrodden miles.

In sunny bays
The young shark plays,
Among the ripples and nets of light;
And the conch-shell crawls
Through the glimmering halls
The coral builds for the Infinite.
And every gem
In His diadem,
From flaming topaz to moon-hushed pearl,
Glitters and glances
In swaying dances
Of waters adream like the eyes of a girl.

The sea and the stars,
And the ghostly bars
Of the shoals all bright 'neath the feet of the moon;
The night that glistens,
And stops and listens
To the half-heard beat of a timeless tune.

Here Solitude
To itself doth brood,
At the furthest verge of the reef-spilt foam;
And the world's lone ends
Are met as friends,
And the homeless heart is at last at home.

HOMEWARD BOUND

Across the scarce-awakened sea,
With white sail flowing,
And morning glowing,
I come to thee—I come to thee.

Past lonely beaches
And gleaming reaches,
And long reefs foaming,
Homing—homing
A-done with roaming,
I come to thee.

The moon is failing,
A petal sailing,
Down in the west
That bends o'er thee;
And the stars are hiding.
As we go gliding
Back to the nest—
Ah! back to thee.

BEATUS VIR

Happy is the man who loves the woods and waters,
Brother to the grass, and well-beloved of Pan;
The earth shall be his, and all her laughing daughters—
Happy the man.

Never grows he old, nor shall he taste of sorrow,
Happy at the day's end as when the day began,
Yesterday forgotten, unshadowed by To-morrow,—
Happy the man.

Fellowed by the mountains, ne'er his heart is lonely,
Talked to all day by rivers as they ran.
The earth is his love, as he who loves one only—
Happy the man.

His gossips are the stars, and the moon-rise his tavern;
He who seeks a better find it if he can—
And O his sweet pillow in the ferny cavern!
Happy the man.

A WALKING SONG

With a Shakespeare in my pocket, and an English briar,

With a brook to run beside me, and the morning at its spring,
With the climbing road before me, and the mountains catching fire,
I feel as I imagine it must feel to be a king.

Be it April or October, wild-rose or silk-weed pod,
The larch's tender green, or the maple's bannered gold,
With my briar for my comrade, and my Shakespeare for my god,
I wonder what the people mean that talk of growing old.

"The Muses love the morning," wrote Erasmus long ago,
And the only place to meet the gods is on the hills at morn;
There still the sacred asphodel, and mystic myrtle grow,
And Memnon sings with joy, because another day is born.

O up into the radiance, for ever on and on,
Be it hoar-frost on the pasture, or blossom on the vine,
With a briar breathing incense, and a song to lean upon,
A song from "As You Like It"—is to lead the life divine.

RECANTATION

I have loved women's faces
Time and again,
But I would rather be
Somewhere at sea,
With the foaming sea-laces,
The sea without stain,
Than all the embraces.

I would rather watch a river flowing.
Or a wild-rose blowing,
Or the swallows that skim,
Or the fish as they swim;
I would rather watch the moon rise,
Or the coming of morn,
Than look in the eyes
Of woman born.

I would rather watch the wild bees
All my days,
And give God the praise,
Than woman and her ways.

THE CLOISTER

I would be left alone with this great love
That is upon me for eternal things;

Come not between me and this passionate hour—
I would not gather any mortal flower;
I would stay thus all day, nor ever move
Nearer to aught that limitation brings.
I crave no friendly touch of outstretched hands.
Nothing that loves again or understands.
Almost too much of meaning hath this stream,
Too near to music; yea, and yonder birds
Too near to human loving for my dream,
That hath not hands nor feet, nor thoughts, nor words.
I would have nothing nearer me than trees,
Nearer to understanding than the hills,
Nearer to loving than the stars or seas.

VII

BALLADE AGAINST THE ENEMIES OF FRANCE

(François Villon)

O may he meet with dragons belching fire,
Like Jason, he who sought the fleece of gold;
Or to a beast, till seven long years transpire,
Like Nabugodonozor, king of old,
Be changed; or smitten with as vast a woe
As Helen's rape brought Troy-town long ago;
Or swallowed be within those bogs of hell
Where Tantalus and Proserpina dwell;
More than Job's sorrows be his evil chance.
Close-snared as Daedalus of whom men tell.
Who could wish evil to the realm of France!

Four months head-downward in the marsh's mire,
Even as the bittern may he cry; or, sold
To the Grand Turk for cash, in harness dire,
Toil like a bull; or, as the tale is told
Of Magdalen, for thirty long years go
Sans wool or linen—yea! unvestured so;

Drowned like Narcissus be he; or, as befel
To Absalom, hang by the hair; 'twere well
Judas' dread end were his, or circumstance
Of horror strange as Simon Magus' spell,
Who could wish evil to the realm of France!

Were but Octavian king—runs my desire—
With molten coin, so slowly growing cold,
To fill his belly; or might he expire
Between revolving mill-stones crushed and rolled,

Like good Saint Victor; or in the choking flow
Of ocean drown, fate worse than Jonah's know
In the great whale; him from thy light expel,
Phoebus; and, Venus—punishment more fell—
Deny him thy sweet self; and ii outrance
Curse him. High God, with curse ineffable
Who could wish evil to the realm of France!

ENVOI

Prince, may Eolus forth on winds compel
His soul, where, sunk beneath the ocean's swell,
The woods of Glaucus gloom, and never glance
Of hope can fall—in him what good can dwell
Who could wish evil to the realm of France!

AFTER THE WAR

After the war—I hear men ask—what then?
As though this rock-ribbed world, sculptured with fire,
And bastioned deep in the ethereal plan,
Can never be its morning self again
Because of this brief madness, man with man;
As though the laughing elements should tire,
The very seasons in their order reel,
As though indeed yon ghostly golden wheel
Of stars should cease from turning, or the moon
Befriend the night no more, or the wild rose
Forget the world, and June be no more June.

How many wars and long-forgotten woes
Unnumbered, nameless, made a like despair
In hearts long stilled; how many suns have set
On burning cities blackening the air,—
Yet dawn came dreaming back, her lashes wet
With dew, and daisies in her innocent hair.
Nor shall, for this, the soul's ascension pause,
Nor the sure evolution of the laws
That out of foulness lift the flower to sun,
And out of fury forge the evening star.

Deem not Love's building of the world undone—
Far Love's beginning was, her end is far;
By paths of fire and blood her feet must climb,
Seeking a loveliness she scarcely knows,
Whose meaning is beyond the reach of Time.

Friend of an art that is the whole world's friend,
A whole world brings its laurels and its tears,
And love amazing—love, the busy years,
Inured to the long loss, that none may mend,
Of the diurnal multitudinous dead,
Pause but how seldom from their tasks to bring
To any laurelled head.
Surely to no mere king,
Or cold achievement seated on a throne,
Wearing the golden armour of its fame,
Such sorrow ever came.

Frohman, some nobler thing
We mourn the loss of, mourning thus for you,
Than any deed or any power to do,
Something we hardly knew
Till that last moment of your going hence,
With those strange words so simply on your tongue,
Words that affirmed beyond all powers of song
The soul's magnificence.

O in a book 'twere wisdom easy said,
Or in some poplar-whispering academe,
Where all man's doings turn into a dream—
"A beautiful adventure"—to be dead;
Or, in long pauses of one's dying breath,
To turn some splendid compliment to death.
But you no leisure had, or warning given,
The stable world yawned to an instant grave;
You, looking on the gulf that hell had riven,
First thought of little frightened lives to save,
Then on the opening doors your quiet gaze
You turned, and, like a player, took your call.

Ah! he who said "the readiness is all,"
In all his tale of man's heroic breath,
Hath no such readiness as this to tell
Of any soul and death.
"The beautiful adventure!"—to take leave
Like that!—we grieve, yet cannot grieve
For that poised soul, who, through the common ways
Of the world's business, carried all his days
That thought eternal, ready all the while
To greet the mystic summons with a smile.

And you, O world that mourns him, bethink, too,
That he who left that challenge there for you
To make a bright beginning of the end,
Was neither priest nor poet—but the friend

Of player-folk, of many theatres lord,
A play-house man, of piety abhorred.

A MERRY BALLAD OF CHRISTMAS

With old familiar sign,
The festival divine
Ruddies the snow-clogged way;
Butchers and toy-shops flame,—
Because the Lord Christ came
To wash our sins away.

Without 'tis merry, snowing,
A-roaring and a-blowing;
Within the wine is flowing,
And men and maids are jolly,
With mistletoe and holly—
Because the Lord Christ gave
Himself our souls to save.

Yet, underneath the singing,
The fiddling and the flinging,
A thought I cannot still
Stalks like a guest unbidden,
Steals like a secret hidden,

Laying its fingers chill
Upon the heart of mirth
That laughs for Jesu's birth—
(Fie on such melancholy,
With mistletoe and holly!)

From an old book I read,
Somewhere within my head
The story lingers
Of a grim castle-hold,
In dreaming days of old
And knights and singers.
And ladies clad in vair,
And a great feasting there,
Torches and swords in air:
Then, in some lull of mirth,
From far beneath the earth,
Came there a wailing—

The wind was it? wailing—
A voice of woe so vast
It held the feasters fast:
So might the lost in hell

Pierce, for a little spell,
The peace of Paradise
With uncouth cries. . . .

Once more the feasters laughed,
Cozened their feres and quaffed,—
'Twas but the knaves that lay.
Far from the light of day,
Beneath their dancing feet,
Rotting and raving,
Chained down with rats and slime,
Lost out of space and time—
(Souls not worth saving!)
So kept they Lord Christ's day,
In the time fled away.

What was my thought, though?
Hearken the whispering snow
Against the pane—
Lord Christ! the wind doth blow
A wild refrain;
Louder, O music, play,
Nimbler, O dancers, glide. . . .

Nay! music cease to play.
Dancers a space abide—
Hearken yon wailing!
The wind is it—wailing?

Nay 'tis the folk that lie
Out in the night there.
The men that starve and die
Far from the light there;
From oubliettes of pain,
From wheel and rack and chain,
Beneath your dancing feet,
Tripping so fleet, so sweet,
From folk that rave and rot,
Forsaken and forgot,
Comes the wild wind's refrain,
Comes all that wailing—
To-day, as long ago,
Long as the wind shall blow.
Long as the snow shall snow. . . .

(But merry is the street,
And merry is the hall,
And a Merry Christmas, gentles all!)

High at a window on the nineteenth floor,
We talked, my friend and I. Across the way,
The iron frame of one new building more
Grew as we watched it, with incessant scream
Of hoisting engines, iron chirp and drone.
Like giant crickets, 'mid the steel and stone.
Of rivet-drivers, pounding shaft and beam;
And through the mighty hubbub something gay
Throbbed like a tune, and held one like a dream.

Pipe in his mouth, with nonchalant sure feet.
One stood above the roaring dizzy street.
Back to the gulf, with careless jesting face.
Waving directions to the engineer,
Swinging a girder gently into place;
And from a smithy, glowing there in space.
Another to a laughing lad below,
Straddling a narrow rib of the gaunt frame.
Tossed rivets white and molten—like a game—
Pitcher and catcher; cigarette on lip,
A battered bucket—if his hand should slip!—
The lad holds out; like two clowns at a show.
Spinning their hats as though the skill were nought,
The flaming bolts from one to the other go,
Light as a feather in the bucket caught.
So bees work 'mid the hum and roar of hives.
Each at his task.

My friend said: "Do you know
For each such building men must lose their lives?
It is as sure, almost as sure, as though.
When the contractor figures out the cost,
So many tons of pressure floor by floor,
He wrote—'So many lives of workmen lost.'
Of course, the figures vary, less or more,
But always some of these poor lads must die,
Before the topmost story scrapes the sky."

Silent, we watched again the man up there,
Perched on the edge of nothing, like a fly,
Jesting across his precipice of air,
And wondered if he'd be the one to die,
We watched the bucket, in a kind of dream,
Catch the candescent bolts the smithy flings,
As though his fellow tossed him some ice-cream—
He lights another cigarette, and sings.

"Always the human sacrifice!" I said—
And "I remember somewhere to have read

How in old Greece and Rome, and later, too,
When they would build a temple or a tower—
Things that we go to gaze on, I and you,
Still, in their ruins, lovely as a flower—
In the foundations, that the work might thrive,
Smiled on by gods above and gods below,
They sometimes buried some poor soul alive—
Much the same thing, though that was long ago!
Yes! there's a bridge in France that spans the Rhone,
With lordly arches of immortal stone,
Repairing which, 'tis said, some workmen found
A seated skeleton of crumbling bone,
There in a little chamber in the ground,
Guarding with eyeless eyes the bridge's gate;
Thus was the bridge made safe, the augurs said,
The Gods of Darkness thus propitiate,
For feet of living wayfarers to tread.

The human sacrifice! Now, just as then,
Here by the Hudson, as there by the Rhone,
These haughty towers on bones of broken men,
Climb to the sky, and glitter in the sun;
Beneath the ball-room floors dead workmen lie,
Light feet above their nameless ashes glide,
No one remembers when or how they died:
A foot that slipped, a long despairing cry,
A hurrying ambulance with icy clang,
A muffling sheet, through which the warm blood drips—
Ah! that young voice that from the girder sang. . . .
This cigarette still smoking from his lips!"

OUR LADY OF PITY

Man of new wonders ever loves to tell:
The ship that sails the air; the voice that flies
Across a world, at touching of a bell;
The picture that shall flash for unborn eyes
The deeds and dances mote-like in the sun
Of us that live now, and so soon are gone—
Each radiant step that from the dark ascends
The star-lit ladder of the climbing brain;
The patient will that to its purpose bends
The dread immortals to a mortal gain,
Turning old terrors into magic friends,
Making a toy of thunder . . .
. . . but most my thought
Ponders on marvels man has half forgot—
The far beginnings of these shining ends;
And, chief of these, when pity first began—

That strange, far moment when another's woe
Stirred in the brutish clay yet scarcely man,
And the first tear was shed—how long ago!—
And lips uncouth first stammered love's first word,
Strange as the first far song of the first bird.
Surely it was a woman, as she pressed,
Unknowing why she loved it, to her breast
The babe so strangely hers, so softly curled
There in her arms; the little flickering flame
That out of blackness into being came
To her, 'mid all the welter of the world.

And, maybe, looking on her tenderness,
Man's fierceness stumbled to a rough caress;
Till lo! this marvel through long ages grew—
Man learned a kindness for the thing he slew.

Mother divine! yea, even now as then
Save us with pity from a world of men;
For, now as then, with war and weeping wild,
Woman has still the whole sad world for child.

ELIXIR VITÆ

So much must I forego that once did make
A keen and racing music in my blood:
No more at founts of passion may I slake
The spirit's thirst, nor all fair things for food
With appetite of youthful lust devour;
Nor speed to fiery ends, nor soar in flame;
Nor crowd all gain and loss into an hour;
Nor shake a universe to build a name.

Age lays its muting fingers on the strings.
Yet, in the silence, something inward sings,
And something sees with strangely wakened eyes;
Time, like a chemist, from the past distils
An essence by whose might the spirit flies
Swift as a shooting star along the hills.

WHEN I AM VERY OLD

When I am very old and none there is
To lift their lips to mine, a flower's cup,
When I have drunken all life's vintage up,
And none shall find me good to see or touch,
And only Death shall find me good to kiss;

I think I shall not sorrow overmuch,
So long as April bares her flowering breast
In secret woodlands, and, with eyes of dew,
Lies to the others as once to me and you!

THE WORLD IS STILL A SONG TO ME

The world is still a song to me,
A little sadder grown,
Less of the lark in it, maybe,
More of the undertone
Of wind and sea.

The surge of Time, the to and fro
Of restless, radiant things,
Flowing along as rivers flow,
For ever taking wings,
Eager to go.

Yet no less sweet upon the tongue
The words of the old tune,
Though every May that comes along
Is all too swiftly June—
Still, still a song!

WHEN I AM GONE

When I am gone, over the silent sky
The birds will fly—
Ah! how the birds will sing
When I am gone;
And the blue eye
Of some unborn and beautiful young thing
Will watch them fly,
And her young heart will break to hear them sing—
When I am gone.

TWO LOVERS

(To Howard and Lucy Hinton)

The loveliest lovers that I know
Wear on their heads two crowns of snow;
It is a fashion of the hair
Upon their heads both brave and fair.

Their beauty, more from day to day,
Time gave, but cannot take away.
A girlish bloom her face still wears,
But no girl in a thousand years
Had ever yet a face like hers;
Nor any youth at twenty's prime
Glanced like this emperor of Time.

Ah, girl, entranced before your glass,
If but for you the years shall pass
As for this twain, you need not fear
For all this beauty now so dear;
For it shall grow a fairer thing.
Now 'tis a blank unmeaning page,
That doth but callow boys engage;
The nobler meanings Time shall bring,
The lovely writing of the soul,
As on some bright illumined scroll,
Shall tell a golden story there;
And lovelier still your face shall be,
Of lasting sweets the honeyed hive,
Though you should then be eighty-three,
And he, your love, be eighty-five.

ON GROWING OLD

Growing old—did you say?
Well, if years must be told,
I suppose one is old;
For this surely is gray
That as surely was gold,
And one's years in the sun
Grow fewer to run;
Where you dream, I have done,
Where you fight, I have won—
If that's to be old.

But, is this to be old?
To love like a boy,
To drink all the joy
Of the green and the blue
Of the earth, like a toy
Made of wonder and dew;
To taste all things new,
As the newest of moons,
As the latest of tunes,
As the brightest of spoons;
To find all things magic—
Laughing or tragic—

All marvel and mirth,
Nothing else on the earth—
Nothing common or stale;
Life all nightingale,
All rainbow and rose,
All song and no prose;
All dreaming of dreams,
And running of streams;
And death a new star
Drawing near from afar—
Is that to be old?

VIII

THE POET

Lover of women and of words,
Driven the wind's way north and south,
Be-fooled by blossoms and by birds,
He wanders with his singing mouth;
Yet wanders not, nor yet is driven,
Nor yet be-fooled in any wise,
For unto him a chart is given
Of all the stars in all the skies.

What matters if his feet shall stray,
Where small pedestrians keep the track.
When, with light tread,
And laughing head,
He firmly walks the Zodiac,
Going his own appointed way;
For never ship upon the sea
Was half so sure of port as he.

Disaster and despair he drinks
As men in taverns drinking wine,
For him the lower the sun sinks
So much the earlier shall it shine,
And all the world be blue with morn.
For this strange reason was he born:
Out of his folly to be wise,
Out of the bitter to bring sweet.
To sing into a Paradise,
And fill it full of dancing feet,
The saddest heart, the blackest street.
And striving always in a dream
Word after word secure to place
In the built music of his scheme,
The mystic pattern of his verse;

To match them with a woman's face,
Or with the ghostly Universe.
Always the words! as he who tries,
With his stern finger, string by string,
The wood his bow shall make to sing,
And with one stroke mount up the skies.
Always the words—the words—the words,
Lovelier to listen to than birds,
And fairer in their shape and hue
Than any flowers that April knew:
Always the woman and the words,
And always folly,
And melancholy.

So poets born must, too, be made,
And so their songs shall never fade.

OLD SAFETY

Delight and Danger hand in hand
For ever dance with dizzy feet,
Old Safety ever hugs the land,
His only care to sleep and eat.

To little gods that rule the mart
He pays his dues and bows his knee,
But gods that bless and break the heart—
He scarcely knows that such gods be.

What though with glory and with awe
Man's little lot be magnified,
He keeps the letter of the law,
His skin is safe, whate'er betide.

For him no rainbow of romance.
No leap into the arms of joy,
No dazzling partnership with chance,
No Helen, and no burning Troy.

The hallowed dream, the flaming bliss,
That fill the souls of those who dare,
Though on the edge of the abyss.
To love—and fall they know not where.

The wildness that alone is wise,
That swoops and takes, and asks no leave
Of gods or men—all for the eyes
More lovely far than morn or eve.

All glories of the lonely deed
Men do for dreams, and, dreaming, die;
Heroes that for a country bleed.
Or Freedom—^like a starry sky.

All souls that fling themselves on fire,
Or on the gleaming lances run,
Martyrs of some divine desire
For others sought, for others won.

Yea! not as these is he who hides
And hoards his being, safe and small,
Far from the elemental tides;
And, living so lives not at all.

Dust unto dust! such dust as he
Insults the procreative sod,
That, sandy desert though it be,
Somewhere with palms gives thanks to God.

This dust shall never flame or flower,
Nor answer to the kindly spring,
Nor any resurrecting power
Breathe life into this lifeless thing.

Safe lived he—safe, being dead, he lies,
Forgotten of life for evermore,
One with the dead who do not rise,
The souls God needs not any more.

ON PROFESSORS

Professors, with their foolish brows,
Pass and depart,
Learnèd in every lore besides
The human heart.

Laughed at by ever-living youth,
Up discreet sleeves,
Selling themselves to teach old lies
No man believes.

Poor dust, called men, that need not die
To be forgot,
That, even living, were as though
They still were not.

Fools stuffed with wisdom as a goose
Is stuffed with spices,

Yet cautious hypocrites, the while,
Of furtive vices.

How long shall youth and strength be slaves
To men like you—
With wild-haired April in the land,
All stars and dew!

THE REAL BOOKS

O take away these books that tell
The hideous so-called truth of things,
These little documents of hell;
Bring us the book that dreams and sings,
And whispers "all is well".

The beautiful is just as true.
And truer, perhaps, when all is told.
Than all this dross and dirt that you,
With little maggot eyes, behold—
Are there not roses too?

Dull pedants of the seamy side
Of Earth's fair robe of stars and flowers,—
Life is a stream where glories ride
'Twixt singing banks a-gold with towers,
Trumpets and pennoned pride.

Give US the book that flowers and flames
With Love and Youth and noble tears,
Great Life, with all its laurelled games;
Give us again the "Musqueteers"—
And keep your Henry James.

ROBERT BROWNING

So many books are gone, lost in the mind,
Nurture forgotten; once on fancy's tongue
Sweet to the taste; many a honeyed song,
Yea! and deep-thoughted fruit with bitter rind:
Browning goes not. As when a boy, I find
Still the old magic master loved so long;
Here still the strength that still can make me strong,
Still the delight of mountains still behind;

And still, among the rocks and stars of speech,
The sudden silver singing of a bird,

Perched on the craggy ridges of his thought,
Too high 'twould seem to sing—still out of reach
Of the world's ear, that hardly yet hath caught
The music hidden in the gnarled word.

A PLEA FOR THE OLD MUSIC

(To André Polah)

Play me some old gavotte,
Or minuet—
To-day I would forget,
And live in the Forgot:
I want to hear the dead folk dancing,
I want to see the dead eyes glancing,
I want dead ladies and dead lords,
The wigs, the furbelows, the swords;
I weary of the sansculotte,
The unkempt northern hordes.
That pour their muddy streams
Across our dreams,
Fouling the sacred fire
With bestial desire.
Knowing no law
Only to glut the sensual appetite,
Or cram the brutish maw.

Yea! Master of the magic strings,
Bring back the fair old-fashioned things,
The gallant bows, the curtseys sweeping,
Of that brave world that's gone a-sleeping,
Where love was none the less a passion
Because fine manners were the fashion.

Play me some old gavotte,
I weary of the carmagnole,
I weary of the sansculotte,
With his Pan-Slavic "soul"—
Bring back pavane and rigadoon,
And Watteau and the rising moon.

ON THE PASSING OF GREEK AND LATIN

(To Michael Monahan)

So THE last strongholds fall, the mob sweeps on!
The mock and scorn of small mechanic brains,

Soon shall the solemn symbols all be gone,
The vessels hoarding the long human gains,
The stored elixirs out of chaos wrung,
By the great dead who fought and dreamed and sung.

For Man, half salesman grown and half machine,
Of Homer's marble speech hath need no more,
He knows not what those mighty accents mean
Caught from the gods along the Attic shore,
Nor of that Roman bronze which Virgil spake
May his shrunk soul the large impression take.

For him enough the language of the mart,
The speech of hucksters wrangling o'er their trade;
The lexicons of the deep human heart
Were for a mightier breed of manhood made,
Men that lived history for Thucydides,
Or at street corners talked with Socrates.

Yea! it is well—for men so small as we
Tongues so imperial have too large a style;
What deeds to fill these robes of majesty,
What thoughts have we, that know but to de-file
The altars of our fathers, and to break
Perfections Time so long hath toiled to make?

Even the tongues we speak for our concerns,
The paltry business of our little day,
Too noble are—he knows enough who learns
In "Esperanto" how to spell his way;
What do we with the speech of gods and kings,
Or tender talk of Heliconian springs?

A SONG OF DYING WORDS

Alas! for the brave words that pass away,
That soon must lose their purple and their gold,
Be on men's lips no more to sing or say,
In no man's book be writ, tale that is told,
Or poem decked, as a white hand with rings,
With such forgotten words as "queens" and "kings".

Soon to be gone like legendary birds,
Flamingo-winged—O drab and desert sky!—
No more shall "lady", loveliest of words,
Answer to "lord": for these great words must die;
Nor "gentleman", that had so brave a sound,
In aught save mouldering lexicons be found.

Or "manners", or good words of like intent,
"Gentleness", "reverence", and "humility"—
Yea! men shall ponder what such words once meant;
And even so staunch a word as "comrade" be
Turned from its loyal use, itself to lend
To every bloody and tyrannic end.

And "vine" and "vineyard" and the purple "grape",
That in their mention sooth our mortal lot,
Shall be no merrier to the ear than crape,
And kindly Dionysus be forgot;
And even the "pipe" that brings the spirit peace
Seem antique and mysterious even as these.

Yea! all the words of glory and of cheer,
To which the hearts of men were wont to dance,
Shall fall no more upon the purged ear;
Discrowned shall go the kingly word "romance",
And glad am I that I was born in time
Still to weave "love", not "lust", into my rhyme.

THE LAST REFUGE

I bought a cave of late in a lone isle,
With pillared dome of glittering stalagmite,
Driven thereto, a lorn distracted wight,
By men that earth and air and sea defile,
A being whom the vulgar times compel
To be a troglodyte—
Leaving the noise and glare of things behind.
Dim corridors far down to Hades wind:
Perchance some gleaming fairy folk from hell
May come a-singing up from underground,
Naked as flowers, with silver asphodel
And wreaths of laurel crowned,
Lordly of limb and blinding fair of face,
To banquet with me in that lonely place,
There shall i sit and let the world go to,
And sometimes, while yet sleeps the noisy crew,
Ere the first air-ship blots the morning star,
I shall steal softly up to my blue door,
And gaze on my lost comrades from afar—
Earth, sea and sky, once mine, but mine no more.

LEAVE US THE STARS

(À propos the threatened communication with Mars)

Leave us the stars!
This world has noise enough
Without the roar of Mars—
Rob not the holy spaces of their calm,
Bring us no idle gossip of the spheres,
Nor desecrate the psalm
That on still nights into our burdened ears
Pours its mysterious balm.

Soon shall the air-ship blot the rising moon,
With vulgar flight across the evening sky;
In vain shall tortured ear and tortured eye
Flee from pursuit of each last silly tune,
And each new fashion of deformity
In vain seek sanctuary
On dawn-kissed peaks of unascended snows,
Or in some isle the sea
Hath kept a secret from eternity,
Hid in her bosom like a lover's rose.

Leave us the stars—O wizard, let them be!
'Tis not for thee
Their white immortal signals to translate;
Thinkst thou their beams tread all those million stairs
For idle prate
With us on our affairs?
Nor strive to flash our foolishness to them:
Leave them unstained the midnight to begem
With astrologic gold,
Leave them to sing at morning as of old—
Yea! unless, verily, thy science dares
Some better way to reach them with pur prayers.

BEAUTY

What meaning hath she—Beauty? like the moon
Casting her magic with indifferent hands
Alike on evil, and alike on good,
Mysterious boon,
Magic beatitude,
Not all our hoarded wisdom understands;
Hinting we know not what, still nothing telling,
Alike in orchards and in charnels dwelling;
Dowering with shapes of glory rose and girl.
Alike, with feet of pearl,
O'er pits of slime in iridescence dancing,
Making of inward foulness outward fair,
Lending to shapes of hell the morning grace

Of innocence entrancing;
Masking pollution with a woman's face,
Hiding, with subtle snare,
The crouching tiger 'neath a woman's hair.

In high cathedrals, where the god-head dwells,
Staining hushed altar-steps with colours holy
Of painted windows, and with hallowed bells,
And mystic music, wholly
Lifting the kneeling spirit to the skies.
On blossoming gardens and on happy fields,
On breasts of birds and wings of butterflies,
On blood-red sunsets over broken shields,
Her wand of wonder lies.
No less than quiet dawns and rising moons,
Volcanoes and typhoons
Deck in her splendours, terribly adorn,
Tenderly flame in all her softest hues;
And corpse-sown battle-fields are hung with dews—
Yea! death she makes as fair as being born.
What meaning hath she?
He who nearest stood
To Beauty's throne hath named her one with Truth—
"Beauty is Truth, Truth Beauty": holds it good,
Think ye, this guess divine of priestly youth?
Yea! is she not the mystic manual sign
On all the works of the unknown Divine
That evermore mysteriously He makes—
That evermore mysteriously He loves
All vessels of His making;
That in His Universe are no mistakes,
And no forsaking?
Even as some master potter in Cathay
Fires in his finished masterpiece of clay
His emblem there that he, the master, wrought it,
And answers for his work till Judgment Day
To him who, coming after, shall have bought it;
So Beauty—may it be?—
Is like the potter's mark, the mystic sign
God placed for man to see
That all his work is one and all divine—
Though that be mystery—
Yea, Death as Life, and grief as joy, are fair,
And wrong as right, the evil and the good,
All gathered up in one beatitude—
Beauty! Lo! there and there!

Take no shame that still I sing the rose
And the young moon, and Helen's face and spring;
And strive to fill my song with sound of streams
And light of dreams;
Choosing some beautiful eternal thing,
That ever comes like April—and ever goes,
I have no envy of those dusty themes
Born of the sweat and clamour of the hour—
Dust unto dust returning—nor any shame have I,
'Mid sack of towns, to ponder on a flower:
For still the sorrow of Troy-town is mine,
And the great Hector scarce is dead an hour.

All heroes, and all lovers, that came to die
Make pity's eyes with grief immortal shine;
Yea! still my cheeks are wet
For little Juliet,
And many a broken-hearted lover's tale,
Told by the nightingale.
Nor have I shame to strive the ancient way,
With rhyme that runs to meet its sister rhyme,
Or in some metre that hath learnt from Time
The heart's own chime.
These ways are not mare old
Than the unmeditated modern lay,
And all those little heresies of song
Already old when Homer still was young.

Richard Le Gallienne – A Concise Bibliography

My Ladies' Sonnets and Other Vain and Amatorious Verses (1887)
Volumes in Folio (1889) Poems
George Meredith: Some Characteristics (1890)
The Book-Bills of Narcissus (1891)
English Poems (1892)
The Religion of a Literary Man (1893)
Robert Louis Stevenson: An Elegy and Other Poems (1895)
Quest of the Golden Girl (1896) Novel
Prose Fancies (1896)
Retrospective Reviews (1896)
Rubaiyat of Omar Khayyam (1897)
If I Were God (1897)
The Romance of Zion Chapel (1898)
In Praise of Bishop Valentine (1898)
Young Lives (1899)
Sleeping Beauty and Other Prose Fancies (1900)
The Worshipper of The Image (1900)
The Love Letters of the King, or The Life Romantic (1901)
An Old Country House (1902)

Odes from the Divan of Hafiz (1903) Translation
Old Love Stories Retold (1904)
Painted Shadows (1904)
Romances of Old France (1905)
Little Dinners with the Sphinx and Other Prose Fancies (1907)
Omar Repentant (1908)
Wagner's Tristan and Isolde (1909) Translator
Attitudes and Avowals (1910) Essays
October Vagabonds (1910)
New Poems (1910)
The Maker of Rainbows and Other Fairy-Tales and Fables (1912)
The Lonely Dancer and Other Poems (1913)
The Highway to Happiness (1913)
Vanishing Roads and Other Essays (1915)
The Silk-Hat Soldier and Other Poems in War Time (1915)
The Chain Invisible (1916)
Pieces of Eight (1918)
The Junk-Man and Other Poems (1920)
A Jongleur Strayed (1922) Poems
Woodstock: An Essay (1923)
The Romantic '90s (1925) Memoirs
The Romance of Perfume (1928)
There Was a Ship (1930)
From a Paris Garret (1936) Memoirs
The Diary of Samuel Pepys (Editor)